v

To Tapni and Kay,

from John

JINGLES OF THE HARNESS

By

John McCullen

To my Friends

"Unspoken Words, like treasures, in the mine,
 Are valueless until we give their birth :
 Like unfound gold their hidden beauties shine,
 Which God has made to bless and gild the earth"

John Boyle O'Reilly
(1844 – 1890)

JINGLES OF THE HARNESS
(Poems of a Farmer and Counsellor)

By

John McCullen
B.Agr.Sc.   M.I.A.C.T.

Published by the Author 1999

By the Same Author :
- The Call of St. Mary's (1984)
- The Brass Thimble (1996)

Dustjacket Design by
Peter McCullen

Illustrations by the
Seven Artists Inc.

ISBN 0 9528532 1 3

All rights reserved. No part of this publication may be reproduced in any form or by any means, without the prior permission of the Publisher.

Printed by North-East Printers, Drogheda

COPYRIGHT © JOHN MCCULLEN, 1999

Foreword

In presenting this book of poetry, I have purposely avoided any categorisation into sections, because I prefer surprise, and my life experience is better reflected in a jumble of topics. It has been a series of adventures between people, organisations, places and things, rooted in my own place at Beamore. Thus, the poems do not appear in any chronological order, and land where they fall, rather like a handful of feathers thrown into the wind.

Many of the inspirations have come from being granted the privilege of walking in the shoes of my friends at times of joy or sadness in their lives. When these poems started to get framed, and hung on kitchen walls, I decided to gather the collection that appears in this volume. To do this required many permissions which were given generously by friends, who will recognise themselves, amongst the pages, and to whom I am immensely grateful.

Originally, my idea was to include, perhaps, twenty drawings with the entire collection of poetry, but when I uncovered the talent of the seven artists – Ann, Peter, Ruth, Grace, Lucy, Dermot and Colm, I realised the poverty of such a policy, and have enjoyed the pleasure of watching a variety of contributions painting pictures from my words.

The book could not have happened without the support, enthusiasm and generosity of many people, and I wish to express my special gratitude to Lorraine Collins, who did the typing and layout, North-East Printers, for their craftsmanship, FBD Insurances who sponsored the launch, and my wife Ann, for her understanding, artistry, unfailing loyalty and encouragement.

It is my hope that amongst the feathers thrown to the wind, you will find one to tickle you into laughter, dry your tears, or caress you into peace.

John McCullen
June, 1999

Contents

	Page No.
Sam	2
The Call Of St. Mary's	4
Nancy	6
Dunmore East	8
The Duchess Of Beamore	10
Miss Angela	13
Danny Reilly	16
The Good Samaritan	18
The Frog	20
Jack	22
Moving House	24
To Gerry	26
The Snowdrop	28
Lady Antoinette	29
Summer	30
A Spouses Lament	32
My Dad	34
Confirmation	36
Clonlusk	38
Anthony's Farewell	40

The Farmers Friend	42
The Fallen Icepop	44
The Fish	46
The White Priestess	48
Annagor Silver Jubilee	50
A Visit To Derry	52
The Tall Grey Man	54
Alter Ego	56
To Francis Ledwidge	58
The Palace	60
Onion Man	62
The Chairman's Role	64
Field Rezoned	67
Toledo '88	69
The Dandy Man	71
The Piemaker	74
The Family Face	76
A Fine Day	78
Mother	80
Eucharistic Minister	82
On The Edge	84
Bernard Flynn's Two Legs	86

Colm O'Rourke's Left Leg	87
William	88
Days Of Study	90
Surrogate Mother	92
Wedding Day	94
Ottawa Hills	95
Sea Shells	97
Tom	98
Alone	100
Twenty Fifth Birthday	101
Headmistress	103
Polyandry	105
Treatment At The Health Centre	107
Peter The Painter	108
The Owl And The Pussycat	110
The New Curate	112
Light In The Sky	114
A New Pair Of Eyes	116
Grateful	118
White Rabbit	120
An Irish Colleen	123
Lady In Red	126

Renewal	127
To Joe Rea	128
Penny	130
To Seán Boylan	132
Travelling Aunt	134
Neighbours	137
Qualified	138
Acceptance	140
Well Done Kate	141
Regrets Only	142
Dodo	144
Moving	146
Goodbye Health Centre	147
The Best Boy In The School	149
To Thomas Clinton	151
The Freeman Of Kells	153
Sesquicentennial	155
Sick Child	158
Christmas	161
The Duster	163
Handyman Available	165
A Mother's Lament	166

Conference '83	168
Installation Aid	170
Cowpath	173
Tour Of '85	175
Exam Wish	178
Kilsharvan	179
Sharing	181
The Queen Of Brookville	182
Glencraff	184
Sisters	186
The Egg	188
Energy	190
A Hooley At 40	192
A Man Apart	194
Vincentian	196
Passing Over	197
Legacy	199

JINGLES OF THE HARNESS

By

John McCullen

SAM

Placid, solid, wise and strong,
You worked hard all day long,
Black hair streaked with sweat,
Leather clothes leaked with wet.

When Sulky Biddy ran away,
They brought you out to save the day
And coax her back into the yard,
The blindfold cloth was your trump card.

At Moat Field gate the combine stuck
Narrow wheels sunk in the muck,
Once more your strength was all
The others lacked, for a final haul.

When Moss needed help for hay
On a sunny, threatened, day,
He called you from the well,
Succumbing to his gentle yell.

Your mighty thirst was fun to view
As draughts of water wildly flew
And slobbered on your ancient collar
And Tom get paid a daily dollar

Such likes will not be here again,
Despite the very best of men,
The jingle of the harness is of yore
For Sam, the carthorse, of Beamore.

THE CALL OF ST. MARY'S

Why should a thing of stones and sand,
Such a constant reverence command ?
Why should something dead and still
So many hearts with prayer fulfill ?

Is it a precious work of art ?
A gift carved out with a horse and cart ?
Or the fruit of brawn and brain,
Standing solid in storm and rain ?

Is it because of the Workman's pain,
That this House beckons us back again ?
Is it a memory of some great Priest,
That brings the people to a common feast ?

Perhaps a memory of times gone by,
A creaking pram and a childhood cry,
That smell of incense on a Sunday night,
Calling us back to the candlelight.

All the memories are part of the stone,
St. Mary's Church will stand alone,
As the House of God above,
A place of Joy and Peace and Love.

NANCY

"I will drive the Minx today," said Annie Grimes
While James was telling us nursery rhymes,
"Off with you, then, Queen Anne, like Lucy Locket,"
He winked, and jingled the keys in his pocket.

"Miss Anne Mary Collette, stand out at the side,"
Mother Mary Eustelle would severely chide,
"Orchestral players must practice decorum,
And Loreto hockey is **_not_** about 'floor them'."

The old Parish Priest of Saint Peter and Paul
Raised his bushy eyebrows, fringes and all,
As Nancy arrived with some strange fellow,
Dressed for Mass, in purple, red and yellow.

Salmon will never be the same as before,
Women daggin' sheep, driving tractors, and more,
Men taking orders from a lassie in pants,
"That one wid never have time for romance."

My father was sitting, at home in the sun,
When Nancy drove up, with her hair in a bun,
Announced engagement to a *PLAYACTOR,*
"What's that you said? A drainage contractor?"

This lady has managed to live like a cat,
You know what I mean, nine full lives and all that,
Yet never too busy with kids, golf and farm,
To help out the neighbour, who might suffer harm.

So if ever you seek to find Tir na n-Og,
Or Septuagenarian who's slightly a rogue,
Just look for a kind heart, a bun and a nose,
That will be Nancy, if the eyes are half closed!

DUNMORE EAST

You must come now and see the hut,
Then we will travel on by foot,
Down the counsellor's sheltered strand
And up the hill to rocky land
Where thrifty tufts of pink do cling
And raucous young kittiwakes sing.

Men's cove is a dangerous place
And down below I splashed my face
In risky swimming to the Closh
While fisherfolk forever slosh
About, with corks, with nets and boats
And gaily cut the fishes throats.

Look, John, there is the famous dock
And pier of old red sandstone rock
holding off Atlantic Ocean.
This place reeks of eternal motion
Woven into my very seams
It holds my carefree childhood dreams.

Stand here a moment, let us view
The Convent and the pumphouse new
And down below the travellers go
Away to sea, and Lawlors show
The new shop front all painted white
Inviting us to drink tonight.

For years, I carry Dunmore East
To lift my life, like bread with yeast
A place where everybody knew
Keating, Tritschler and Butlers too,
The loves and laughs and risks I took
Are written fast in my life's book.

THE DUCHESS OF BEAMORE

In the time of Rudyard Kipling and Mark Twain
And a month before the birth of John Wayne
The Duchess arrived in Drogheda town
Dressed in a long white Christening gown.

The road to the Palace was earthy enough,
And the Duke sat by the fire having a puff.
While Mary gathered sticks from acres galore
And the Ballroom fire up the chimney did roar.

Ladies in waiting, be jiminy smack,
Would come and go out the door at the back.
The face of a Christian you rarely would see
They must be all Muslims, except Father J.C.

On Tuesdays and Fridays, the Duchess would roam
Up Shop St. and West St. away from her home,
Nodding to subjects who sought just a glance,
Or perhaps she was seeking a bit of romance?

Her transport was always a welloiled high Nellie
Her task to ensure the Duke a full belly
And when suitors arrived, they never were able
To find the Duchess sitting under the table.

Like the Old Queen she went to the races
Dolled up for the day with hat and black laces,
She usually managed to make a few bob
While the Duke lost his shirt and came home with a sob.

As often as not the audience would queue,
A mixture of emigrants, students, hens, me and you,
All coming to hear the latest news,
Or get a word in edgeways with their own views.

The message will say that her grace is perplexed,
And because of this fuss madam is vexed,
What can loyal subjects do, but call for three cheers
When the Duchess of Beamore reaches 90 years.

So thank you Mary McCullen for all the good times,
For all that you taught us in stories and rhymes,
We're glad that you always kept open backdoor
For all your loyal subjects in Beabeg and Beamore.

MISS ANGELA

I miss your wild medical dreams
Which come and go, like phantom reams
And tell of craggy Dunmore cliffs,
Inhabited by Hospital stiffs.

I miss that vital second cup
Without which, you will not wake up
To face another hectic day
With gentle smile, and winning way.

I miss your tidy welldressed self
Just like some magic woodland elf
Who finds each day a new attire
To keep man's burning flame afire.

And, in my study, as I pore
No cup of tea glides in the door
At eleven o'clock, or at four,
To serve myself – a hopeless chore !

I miss the menu for every meal
The guarantee to make me feel,
That balance in my food shall be
Part of the love of you and me.

I miss your suntanned cheery smiles
To greet me home, from weary miles
To pass the news of many phones
The while I munch the two hot scones.

There is no presence everywhere
Of wife and mother to really care
To give this house a heart and soul
Would seem to be your daily goal.

I miss your constant Action plan
To cater for the little man,
To keep at bay the constant threat,
"Mammy … Mam … are we going yet "?

I miss your gentle parting kiss
Often featured in poems like this,
But greater than the written word,
Is a kiss delivered in accord.

I miss your sudden inspiration
to improve counselling communication
tossing ideas like harvest chaff,
you help to make my captives laugh.

I miss your hand to join in prayer
To solve the troubles that we share
To pass to God worries of the day
So He may clear it all away.

Despite these things I sorely miss
From heated scone to gentle kiss
No time or place can conquer love
Free to fly, like a bird above.

DANNY REILLY

Are you the Danny Reilly
That I knew so long ago
When we worked with Renee
At the Oldcastle Show ?

Or are you the Danny Reilly
That tested for the lime
Way out at Gortloney,
In ould God's time ?

Or perhaps you're the Danny Reilly
With the glint in his eye
That won the Macra Public Speaking
When Adam was a boy ?

Whichever of the three you be
I enclose a gift from me
A thimble made from solid brass
To give to your own wee lass.

THE GOOD SAMARITAN

"Who is this Frank ?" said the man in the street.
"The grandest wee man you ever could meet,"
spoke three voices all the same,
at the mere mention of that name.

A young girl passing thought a while,
"Is that the happy man with the smile ?".
He always had a kind word to say,
Whenever I met him on the way.

Is this the artist with gifted hands
Who helped the sick in foreign lands,
And captured beauty with his strokes
To then give away to other folks…

Who will wind the clock in the sacristy,
Quoth the Parish Priest in his homily,
Who will show us the power of prayer,
Doing hours for others, kneeling there?

Mary, I'm leaving this parcel of stuff,
And Paul, did your shot end up in the rough?
Oh, Gerry, the washing machine needs a belt or a yoke.
Wait Ruth, did you hear my latest joke?

No bagpipe swirled in a lonely dirge,
As clouds and wind and sun did merge
In Calvary's field, a flute and fiddle sang
With bodhran and banjo the music rang.

"Who is this Frank?" said Peter with the key.
The Lord said, "My man by the Boyne, come to Me,
You carried your cross and My will was done,
Come in and be welcome, Frank ould son,
We need saints who can cut a silverside,
Come and meet Mary, Saint Frank of Sunnyside.

THE FROG

On a dewy morning
With no real warning
Trudging down by the brook
A glistening sharp look
Stopped me in my track
And threw my mind far back
To an old childhood story
Of souls in Purgatory.

Perhaps you were a King
Once monarch of everything
Now in total command
Of five square yards of land.
What sin did you commit
To cause you now to sit
In the low Long Leg field
And only me to yield.

Perhaps disloyal priest
Watching sun in the east
Rising over the Boyne
Growing too fond of coin,
The tribute thrown to God,
And siphoned to cod
All the obvious sinners
While you ate full dinners.

Whatever that awful crime
I judge you have done time
Enough to clearly shrive
Your soul. So now, alive,
Hop your way to heaven
Because before eleven
I bless you for battle
And go, counting cattle.

JACK

Happy birthday, my little boy
Today would be a day of joy
Three giddy sisters would help bake
A candled first birthday cake.

Yet still my trembling lip I bite
And brimming salt tears block my sight
A sadness fills my very soul
And panic doth my heart cajole.

Among the painted trees I seek
Recoil from words I cannot speak
Pushing my God to tell me why
You joined Grandad in some sky.

Not many know that you were here
And hold a place so very dear
No paper tells your claim to fame
But gentle love surrounds your name.

MOVING HOUSE
(with apologies to Shirley Valentine)

Goodbye wall, I'll sigh for pastel shades,
While memories of the fireplace fades,
But I'll not miss your hidden words
Of rages, conflicts and sad discords.

By the berried tree, we built a home
And sunk four new walls into black loam,
Fenced it round with iron and wire
To create a hearth with good coal fire.

Nearer to God's heart in garden heat
Where grew one big tree with sheltered seat,
Clematis climbed, and parsley grew,
Forget-me-nots blushed gentle blue.

Where will I be, if I leave all this?
Will I survive, without what I miss?
P'haps I should stay, and live with the wall
And make my own noise to drown it all?

Hello, new wall, and how do you do?
This is myself, and here is my crew,
Can you also hold the Sacred Heart?
And the Blind Piper plying his Art?
Have you space for flickering candle,
Is that too much for you to handle?

TO GERRY

Perhaps, I saw you in some distant way
When I was young and never knew
That your sad death
Would leave a mark on me,
Seeing the nurses tears I said
"This is a man of love".

In a longlost picture and
A missing name, I met
Your mothers sadness and
Lifting a frame tried
To restore her gladness – she said
"My son is a man of love".

In breaking the Bread of Life
I met your wife and thought
Here is something more than
Eyelashes and good apparel
And to her lonely face, I said
This was a man of love.

In an easiness of words
I came to know your daughter
And calming fears, found
A treasury of life. For this,
And your constant blessings
"You are a man of love".

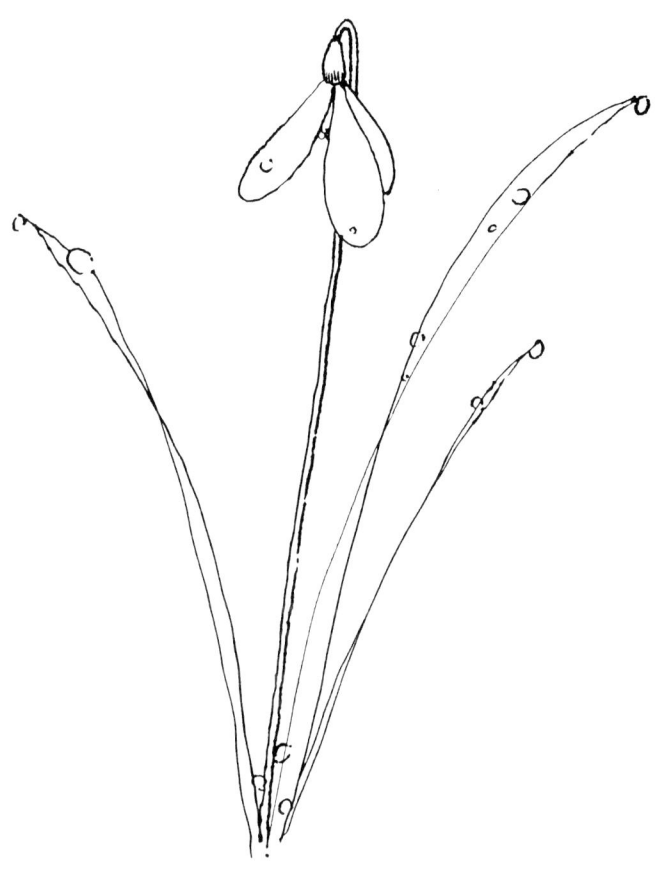

THE SNOWDROP

Green tiny and white
A beautiful sight
Sign of Spring
Everlasting
Memory of childhood
And Brother.

Bowed head prays
East wind sways
Captures the Spring
Glistening
Reminder of God
And Mother.

Window in a cell
Of love will tell
Delicate gift of Spring
Heartwarming
Ode to Summer
And Another.

LADY ANTOINETTE

A bundle of energy flying around
Dainty feet hardly touching the ground
Helping the lame to cross a rough road
Sharing a dying man's heavy load.

Loving us all with a sparkling eye
Never a one to tell a lie
Fighting that truth would set us free
Leaving her mark on Cardinal O'Fiaich.

Laughing with children to leave them at ease
Hiding a loneliness on aching bended knees.
Constantly moving red tape from the system
We are glad she met Brian – and kissed him.

This is the Netta we are proud to know
May Shalom be yours wherever you go
Providing you do what we recommend
A 5 night course – with a Cert. at the end.

SUMMER

I'll smell your fragrance from the beans
As honey waiting for the bees
And see your movements in the barley
Shaking in the dancing breeze.

I'll feel your gentle touch
In slowly walking grassy leas
And hear your voice in lowing cattle
Who pray awhile upon their knees.

I'll sense your wisdom
In the strong, old, trees
And know your love in birds
That fly across the seas.

A SPOUSES LAMENT

Old Neptune blew his wreathed horn
And on that day a new me was born
I became a spouse of a selected kind
And left behind my childish mind.

There used to be time for having a row
But now it's all about the what and the how
And years ago I'd enjoy a huff …
But now it's all conflict-resolving stuff…

God be with the days of throwing a brick
And showing the world that I could be thick,
Concreteness is your only man
So buy shares in CRH while you can.

Once a week I wanted to be real
But only was asked "How do you feel?"
Programmes were made I knew nothing about
And I felt I wanted to scream and shout!

There is a client on yonder hill
And if I don't see him, he'll be there still
So mind the kids and be a honey
There's more to life than making money.

There are times when I can't be sure of my role
The Tutor will know whether I'm broken or whole
The last brainstorming has left me bemused
And after the next one, I'll be totally confused.

Oh, woe is me, I can't be me
Ever since the person joined CMAC
Some of these days I'll struggle free
And flail the lot with immediacy …

I can't tell the name of my own dear spouse
Confidentiality is limited in what it allows
But if you see Clare, or Turlough or Terry,
Tell them I'm a crisis case waiting for Gerry.

MY DAD

A solid man of stubborn mien
Yet rooted in a rural scene
A moral man of prayer and faith
Lost engineer with his lathe.

A man at ease with his soft cap
And rarely ever in a flap
A football match or a fireside tale
Gave more joy than glass of ale.

"A wise man", said young mother
"An eccentric", said another
"A gentleman", said the lady
"He was kind to me", said Brady.

You sat upon the garden seat
Unmoving in the sun,
Why did we keep so many thoughts,
Until your day was done?

CONFIRMATION 1987

The cheeky nose is past and gone
The flirting freckles flown
No longer will you throw a brick
Or call a boy a 'silly thick'.

The trees you climbed are now alone
Mother will no more hear the moan
Of broken limbs and tattered knees
And Flush can rest from many a tease.

The daily struggle with long blond hair,
The dash with Kate for the TV chair,
Are acts we will not ever see,
What can the Bishop's power be?

Mucky boots will now be clean
Teachers will never be "horrid mean",
"I'll never talk to the silly cow"
will now become a respectful bow.

Can a sunny day in May,
Make you see another way?
Or is it grace from the Holy Dove,
That fills the World so much with love?

Whatever it is, a chapter will end
And scissored ear will quickly mend,
This moment is the start of many
Stand back, make way, for the Lady, Jenny.

CLONLUSK

I ploughed seven fields above the rock,
The older neighbours gazed in shock.
Why would that lad break good bullock ground
With that new plough going round and round?

His father left it in forty-five
What would he say if he were alive?
"The 'rale oul' boss id turn in his grave –
the youth today – they won't behave".

I drove on, sou-westered head down
Watching the sod with a puzzled frown;
Why did it not lie solid and flat
And bury the grassy foggy mat?

Yellow Furze sent on a big black cloud
Pulling the coat round like a shroud
I snuggled into the engine tank
And watched the white gulls breaking rank.

They dive at the worms with wild screams
And the ploughboard ever onward gleams,
Throwing flinty soil to the warm sun
And old worms to the birds, one by one.

I must have had something then to prove
To make such a final drastic move
And most of all, upset the neighbours
With Youth's modernistic behaviours.

There were mouths to feed, and wheat to grow,
Indeed, how would old men ever know
That once the right hand was on the plough,
No turning back would my pride allow.

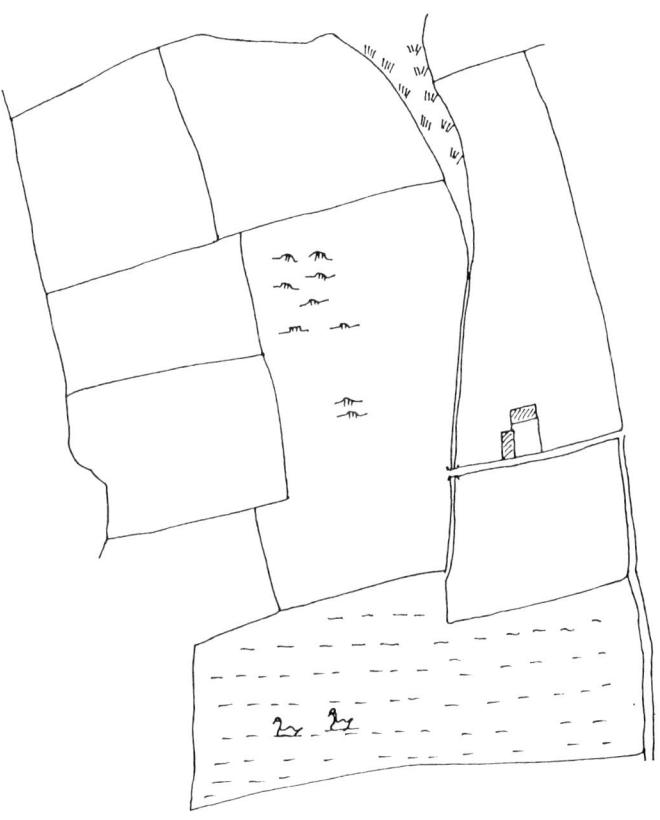

ANTHONY'S FAREWELL

I am sure you smiled at your vacant chair
And rubbed a hand in your thick white hair
Imagine! A woman above in the Park,
And you waiting a lifetime for a Labour mark.

When the Priest intoned, in a solemn way,
"We pray for Mister Hamilton today"
I am sure you smiled at such a phrase
For Anthony, who mixed, with uncommon ease.

As Winnie and the family faced that crowd,
I am sure you smiled, and were quite proud
That a man, who lived for eighty years,
Left adults <u>and</u> children shedding tears.

As you watch our Netta travel that mile
I am sure you smiled a wistful smile
For all the times you had slipped a note,
Into the pocket of a grandchild's coat.

I am sure you smiled at Seans oration,
And blushed a little as he told the nation
About the bottle of Paddy you hid away
To help an old man on a lonely day.

I am sure you smiled when you saw Dick Spring
And turned, and said to the Heavenly King,
"Did I tell you the one about going to the States
or shaving gooseberries, with a friend of Kate's"?

THE FARMERS FRIEND

There was a young man called Gaybo,
Who thought that the farmers had dough,
He reckoned they stored it up in sacks,
And always refused to pay their tax.

Like many young men in Synge Street,
He fancied the farmer grew wheat,
From his mouth, as he milked an old cow,
Surrounded, in kitchen, by bonhams and sow.

As time passed by in his life,
He captured a harp and a wife,
And moved the whole lot to Howth Hill,
While his audience got bigger still.

Even having a job with the N.D.C.,
He still thought that a farmer would flee,
From any sight of soap and water,
Alas, he reckoned without his daughter.

One sunny day, she visited Dad,
Who began to feel like a bit of a cad,
For his darling daughter was going to marry,
A cowman farmer, by the name of Larry.

As years flew by, and grey hairs grew,
Gaybo discovered what he always knew,
About farmers, was all too wrong,
They were just people all along.

And when it came to the last Late Late,
And St. Peter, and Pan, were at Heaven's Gate,
They creaked it open, for doddering Gay,
On the grounds he was a friend of the I.F.A.

THE FALLEN ICEPOP

On a stone outside the backdoor
I sat, the ration books were in,
It was a great day to be four,
Watching the shopping with a grin.

A whole ice-cream wafer to lick
My tongue rambled round the edge
Surrounded by hens, as they pick
Insects and grain under the hedge.

Suddenly a flashing red hen
Grabbed my wafer in her beak,
And I was left bereft, and then,
Trying to stifle rage to speak.

Years flews, I met a mother of three
Pushing a pram up Mary Street
Topics grew between her and me,
The child's ice-pop fell at her feet.

The old red hen flew in my brain
And modern tears fell on the pram.
I knew how to banish the pain …
Would it be misread as a sham ?

Once more, I met mother and three
Presented ice-pops in a rush,
Knew the red hen would forever flee
When Mary said 'thanks', with a blush.

THE FISH

One late summer night, I heard the bell,
A spasm of curiosity over me fell.
With pounding heart, I threw open the door
And – shining outside – was Excalibur,

Patrick held it in his hands
beaten from the waters of many lands
A Salmon shining in grey light
to brighten up the falling night.

"A gift" he said, and proffered it,
a man for whom brevity is the soul of wit.
With much surprise, I took the fish,
my stomach anticipating a tasty dish.

I bore that fish into the hall –
"Why did <u>you</u> get it", shouted All,
with haughty mien, I did them over-rule
"I am seeking Wisdom, like Fionn McCool".

Yet in my head I was the Bible boy,
of loaves and fishes, for Christ to multiply
and loved the symbolism of the gift,
and the Lady who gave our lunch a lift ….

THE WHITE PRIESTESS

Glide on the altar, host in hand,
A slight presence, with strong command,
No rush, no fuss, no numbers game,
Each single person with a name.

Spiritlike, dressed in flowing gown,
Bread of life passed gently down,
This supper is a meal sublime,
Out of season and out of time.

A white host, white soul, pale white dress,
Yet, in that face of loveliness,
Deep eyes framed by hair so dark,
What sadness left this eternal mark ?

Today, God has no hands but these,
The jar of flour will always please
And jug of oil will never dry,
While tended by this deepset eye.

Guide on the altar, host in hand,
No sermon do the crowd demand,
But go their way with happiness,
Fed by a gifted white priestess.

ANNAGOR SILVER JUBILEE

At Annagor, in days of yore
Lived single Mathews men
A bachelor home where servants bowed
And punch and whiskey flowed.

Meanwhile, above at the Gaelic field
The pressure of trespass made Seamus yield,
And with Paddy and Tom, the eternal youths,
He moved, and dug up all his roots.

Ditches fell and hedges flew
And the JCB came mullockin thro'
The unchanged pastures of Annagor
Which saw bagstuff like never before.

When all the cows and machines were humming
Seamus decided he needed a woman
To add a touch of feminine class,
And also drive him out to Sunday Mass.

Now Shelagh was involved in the I.C.A.
And Seamus admired the Kerry way
So before you could say old King Puck,
They were covered in confetti and good luck

In twenty five years of pain and joy
They reared three lassies and a brothy boy
On the banks of the Nanny, facing the sun,
The ghosts of the past were watching the fun.

So here's from all who viewed the game
And from Una and Tom, who ref'd it
We grant them peace and love for free
On this occasion of their Silver Jubilee

A VISIT TO DERRY

I thought to find a terraced wall
Of red, faded British bricks,
With standing men, dogs, kids and all
And splintered bullet holes and nicks.

Instead, there was a peaceful place,
Nestling in the old park of Troy.
Oak trees hiding a gentle face
And one solitary school boy.

Will I fit in her hectic life ?
Is this the Madame Boyle demesne ?
Where indeed are the signs of strife ?
Washed away with drizzling rain ?

The Lady of the Manor comes
Warm, charming, and with Barry's Tea
And instantly the whole place hums,
With special welcome given me.

All work is stopped, and clients dropped,
Maeliosa willingly vanished,
Widow on a sofa flopped,
Till all weary woes were banished.

Truly, a residence of grace
Da Vinci, music in the air.
French windows to the south do face,
A scholar's books are everywhere.

Each little nook a tale to tell
There are prison crosses new and old,
One pressed as a work to sell,
The other fashioned hot and cold.

I slept that night in thirty-three
With strings of beads to block the moon;
This was no traveller's sleep for me
Surprised to be at home so soon.

Treasures of the past were on view
Like footpaths of red, white and blue.
Crossing the bridge, the sidewind blew,
Where crosses stood, and bullets flew.

Time had flown and I said good-bye
To Catherine of the kindly eye
May her heart always be merry
As that time spent in lovely Derry.

THE TALL GREY MAN

I met a child at a party for Mothers.
We both escaped from bigger brothers
And played some childlike games
While distant Aunties called our names.

I met a boy in Palace Street
He wore solid boots upon his feet
And passed the doctors door
Unaware of what lay in store.

I met the Doctor's daughter in a Rathmines flat
And always liked her after that
She little knew, that on Palace Street,
You had marked her out as "pretty neat".

I met a farmer round the table
Who helped me cope 'til I was able
To change from speaking with loud hailer
To putting tons into a trailer.

I met a man in a bed of pain
Locked in a position, again and again,
And found a way to run and walk
By sharing discs and ligament talk.

I met a father in frustration,
Children are the future of the nation
But sometimes aren't as wise as us,
And cause the most unholy fuss ...

I met a tall grey man of fifty
And pray the lord to keep us nifty
For someday soon we'll both have a rest
And catch up on the things we like the best.

ALTER EGO

Soft and wise
With big black eyes
He sits, on yellow tail
And could not fail
But to amuse.

Upon old head
And tum well fed
A purple hat
And waistcoat that
Calls up Lent.

Beak of Babel
And Taiwan label
Telling by one look
He is a happy duck
That lives.

TO FRANCIS LEDWIDGE

Now bugloss pinks the edge of ditches
Sweet woodbine, like an errant child,
Crowns the sloes with riches,
While shyly peep the roses wild.

Marooned in a machine I sat
Gazing over the River Boyne
Rain on the rooftop, pit and pat
Sprinkled wet on the yellow shine.

No trace of tractor smoke or trailer
Coming empty from far-off mill,
The rain has stopped the baler
Making blocks of the strawy hill.

Until this cloud will move along,
I unravel the luncheon box,
Switch on the radio for song,
Watching the slithers of the fox.

All signs suggest the day is down
I read of blackbirds, gypsy June,
The Poet suffered an early crown,
He picked a reed, and made a tune.

Big raindrops fell, and tears came by,
At the loss to the Human Race,
He shall not hear his bittern cry
Young Ledwidge with the laughing face.

Was it for country or for King,
For a lost love or Lord Dunsany
That you followed swallows on wing
And left Donaghmore to be rainy ?

I, alone on the fateful page
Grieving the Boyne's sweet Blackbird still,
Mixing tea, sadness, milk and rage
When Breeda came over the hill
Bearing a basket, food and fruit,
Is it Elie, in her best suit ?

THE PALACE

I built my castle in the air,
A place to rest from sad despair,
Ascending flights of stairs to Heaven
I made my own of Number Eleven.

Renoir adorned the mantlepiece
And incense killed the smell of grease,
Books piled up on the only shelf,
And I began to find myself.

Words hung upon every wall
And each time the bell did call,
I wondered was I really free,
Is this place mine - - and just for me ?

Twixt frozen flush and nibbling mouse
I grew to love that very house,
For here at last, I lost my fears
And on my own, peace conquered tears.

No phone adorned a shining table,
To choose my channels, I was not able,
But lilac perfume came in May,
And kitten's mew did music play.

Farewell, my palace in the air,
The future lies in God knows where,
But strength will come from Number Eleven,
Where I spent Summer eighty-seven.

ONION MAN

"There are seven ages of man" …
Or so the famous Bard began …
Thomas Denis Edward McC. …
Was hit in the eye – by me …
With a popgun … in 1953 …

This is violent, Durcanesque, recollection
A peeling of layers might be a better reflection
First skin to Warrenstown and Brother O' Hare
Who didn't realise hidden talents there.

There lives a Turk somewhere in Spain
Who thinks about God now and again
Because of an argument late in the night
When Eamon decided to put matters right.

The third layer covers a Farm Tasks Quartet
Shaun, Liz and John were relieved when they met
The clearthinking cowman from Elmgrove
Who impressed Judges with the wisdom of Jove.

Macra and the stage provides the fourth layer
Tom Kelly and John Callan were supposed to be there
But the prompting that saved Eamon's skin
Really came from Sheila Murphy and Mary Gavin.

Then came the graceful Lady of Shallot
Determined to carry Eamon to Camelot
Despite the gaspipes, motorways and FEOGA
They have found their own Tir na N-Óga.

Quoth Seamus – 'there was a tree on yonder hill',
It's ploughed up for onions – so it isn't there still …
But when a man reaches two score and ten
And does it better than other men

Let's toast him together before it may pass
Eamon, may there never be a leek in your glass !
And may your corms always be big
And your head be happy – without a wig !!

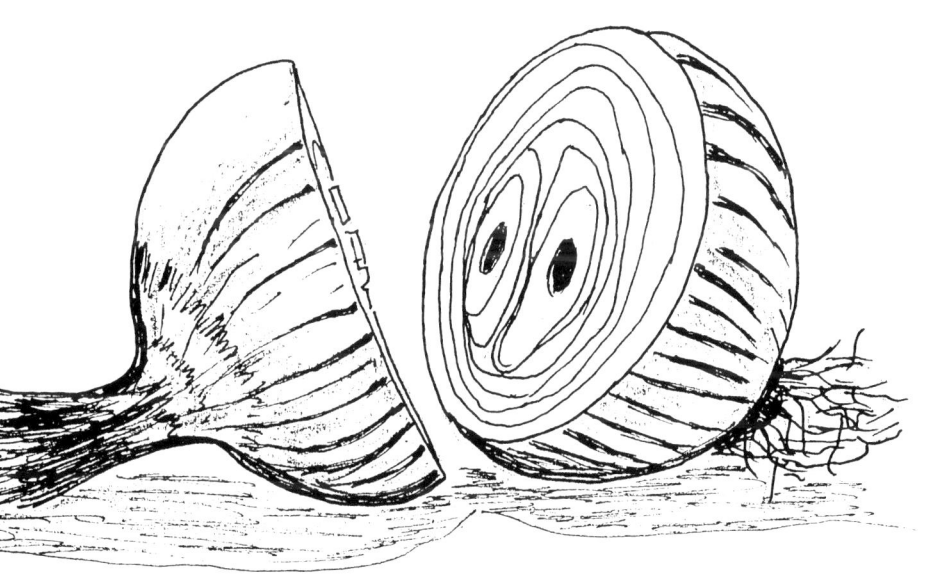

THE CHAIRMAN'S ROLE

On Monday, I called to William Street,
Colleen was ready, tidy and neat.
We drove to Ballyboden for the day,
To hear what the pupils had to say,
And there we met Father Tommy Cooney .….

Tuesday came a Pre-Marriage Course,
Matters are slowly getting worse,
I helped Marie cope with marriage ills
Dealing with sex, drink and pills,
And there we met a Lay Minister .….

On Wednesday, at eight o'clock,
With Netta, I got a bit of a shock,
The boys in Shop Street, took the other pair
And we were left our loss to share,
And there we met Father Tommy Cooney ….

Hello, Mrs. Mac, you are <u>NOT</u> the same,
Have you dyed your hair or changed your name
Since last we met, I'd be willing to bet
That you've grown taller, or perhaps it's smaller ?

Excuse me, now, I am in a flurry !
This isn't the wife ? Oh! don't worry,
I won't breathe a word to the Bishop of Kells,
It won't be me who finally tells ….

Thursday came and a medical talk,
With Sheelagh Wickham I did walk
Before a crowd of one hundred and twenty -
Even Paddy O'Dwyer said he learned plenty
And there we met the Bank Manager's Secretary ….

On Friday morning, I drove to "34"
Pauline was waiting at the door
She must have been feeling in fine fettle,
Because we had coffee in the Copper Kettle
And there we met the Lay Minister ….

Friday afternoon, we checked on the hotel
I began to feel a bit unwell.
When the Receptionist said "A room for two ?"
Pauline turned bright red and blue,
And there we met the Bank Manager ….

On Saturday early, I headed off West,
With Mary Chapman my tutoring to test,
There was lashings of empathy, and custard too,
But you never know who is watching you,
For there we met Father Fox C.C. ….

On the day of rest, Ann came with me
We went for a walk down by the sea,
'Twas there I was held by the Gardaí
On a serious charge of polygamy ….

I am in the court, it is looking sinister,
There in the front is the Lay Minister,
Father Fox C.C., the Bank Man and his Secretary grim,
All with Father Tommy say "That's him" !

"Off with his head", "clap him in the stocks" !
"He's not fit to live", "He should be breaking rocks" !
The Judge non-directive, non-judgemental sentences me
To confidential treatment from CMAC.

FIELD REZONED

Goodbye field, I have known you for a life
And now your days are ended with a knife
Of a bulldozer blade ripping apart
Structure, roots, insects and your very heart.

My foot walked every inch of your clay
In rain, sun, wind, on a foggy day,
And knew the sunken shallow water spring
And where plough shares and rock would ring.

You were contrary, awkward-shaped cuss
Yet we could work together, two of us,
To grow a malt barley fit for brewers,
All captured now for domestic sewers.

The straying sod and the gravelly rocks,
The flint remains, seashells, and old red crocks
Would tell stories, whenever we would meet,
No more ! Alas ! but buried in concrete.

Goodbye, field, we have shared precious time
At least, you are remembered in a rhyme.
I wonder will the new people feel your heart
As Stephen Coyle did, with a horse and cart ?

TOLEDO '88

Ships of wheat just sailed away
While spuds decayed in sticky clay
A five acre farm in Nancy's lane
Offered a life of hungry pain.

The quay was thronged with sad goodbyes
But hope shone deep in many eyes
And Nicholas knew he had to go
To leave behind the Landlord's woe.

Ploughshares crunched through virgin soil,
Handsome houses grew with sweat and toil.
Imagine ! trees for me alone …
And crops the Landlord does not own.

Bright lights beckoned, railroad rattle,
Calling Fern from the crops and cattle,
Grandad risked the daunting sea,
Oil and transport will do for me.

No longer do the spuds decay,
The Landlord's woe has passed away.
Fern and family have found their roots,
With tea, brown bread and welly boots.

As Ruth approaches from the skies,
Hope still shines deep in many eyes.
A small step spans Teddies and clay,
The world is shrinking every day.

THE DANDY MAN

There was a tall thin golly man
Who throve on a diet of Desperate Dan,
He wore his trousers in a flare
And silken shirts over chest so bare.

He brought on board some crazy notions,
Gleaned from Bert over the oceans,
And lashed us with the diamonds four,
As soon as we came in the door.

At first the Tutors had a feeling,
That too much Paris left him reeling,
But when he produced the leather bag,
They knew it was no HQ gag.

You might have come from Cork or Derry,
But there was no time for making merry,
Until the work was done and finished
And energy levels had diminished.

When the Training Team had done their Time,
To the Cooley mountains he would climb,
And breathe the air of bog and pine
Clearing the lungs of Dublin 9.

Bellinter came, and summer days,
To try advanced empathic ways,
And help our clients replace pills,
With doses of knowledge, awareness and skills.

His final fling was on heads and guts,
And a farewell cake from all the nuts,
It surely is a sign of age –
When two nuns push Colm off the stage !

All this now fades into the mind,
Eight years of toil for human kind,
Enlivened by the training Team,
To be specific, you know what I mean !

Our thanks to Colm the Derry Dove,
Taking with him lots of love,
For all the gifts and strengths he gave,
God bless you, Colm, as you take your leave !

THE PIEMAKER

Can I come for a spin in the field ?
Dad ! I promise not to get in the way
No need for wooly hats as a shield
And what job can I do to get pay ?

This sowing is a really slow chore
Please let me free to the outside world
At end of the run, open the door
Oh ! look ! there is a maggot, unfurled.

Can I hide in the bags, while you sow ?
Or perhaps I will play, with the clay
And watch the big black birds come and go,
Is my bar in the box, for today ?

What makes the clay go stuck together
Under the big wheels of the tractor ?
Look ! there is a change in the weather …
When it rains, I am a playactor …

Under the trailer, like farmer's sons,
I have found a great occupation,
Made eleven million hot-cross buns,
And fed the jolly British Nation.

THE FAMILY FACE

"Come in, and be welcome", the Old Woman said
Your Uncle, the Monsignor, buried our dead.
The Lady of the pub said "Pour him a drink"
The Carpenter's Guild has been our common link".

"I will sell you the field" spoke a weary voice.
"Your Grandfather gave us the house of our choice".
"Park your car safe, in here beside the Shelbourne,
Your Godfather did me a lifelong good turn".

"As long as you wish, you can have B. & B.
For the man from Meath was a good friend to me".
"You are sure of a vote from Fianna Fáil
Joe and Thos. helped me when business was small".

"I will not charge a bill for leaving it right
Your Uncle, the Doctor, came often by night".
"I will polish the table, straighten the legs,
Mrs. Mac was a lady who gave me duck-eggs".

"The Board has made it's firm and final offers
'Brother of Pat's ? Well, I'll look in the coffers",
"We do not send reporters, as normal rule …
Who did you say ? A brother of McCool ?"

"Do some research"? said the Trinity Man,
"Related to Dermot ? I'm sure we can".
There is no other ghost I can embrace
But enjoy the haunting of the Family Face.

A FINE DAY

Driving down the crowded street,
One in a million, I chanced to meet.
A spheirbhean with a cheerful smile,
I decided to stop and pause awhile.

In a room wellknown to Bernard Shaw,
We talked of poetry in the raw
And drank a cup of sweetened brew
Such pleasure is given to a chosen few.

At the waiting car, I showed you "Niamh"
A gentle piece, not seen riamh,
And sun shone from a cloudless sky
While men with uniforms passed by.

We bade farewell and you floated off,
Heart uplifted, despite the cough,
I moved my car from the yellow line
And paid the garda the ten pound fine.

MOTHER

You picked me in a ladies choice,
Waltzing round the kitchen floor,
Listening to McCormack's voice,
Float freely in the open door.

When I sought words to cover "fat"
You, wisely, came up with "well - built"
A piece of magic wordplay, that
Washed away all trace of guilt.

Dolly was your normal name
I always thought it very strange
For one who tackled every game
And took the eggs from the hens free-range.

Several careers passed you by
With pen, patient, bowl and flower
For boys to find sea and the sky
And kindness nurturing flower.

At home with a trowel in hand
And private to the very last
You gave us a garden so grand
And a glimpse of a thrifty past.

A life spent with a sweeping brush,
Gathering the dust of others,
At moments when I hear the hush,
I thank you, best of mothers.

EUCHARISTIC MINISTER

I sat in fresh straw
Pondering in awe
At the power of presence
Or some kind of essence
That lingered in the place
Days beyond your feet and face.

Unusual birthday this, but real
My back against the trailer wheel
Sun breathing on my skin
Combine distant with it's din
Insects usually named as pests
Come today as welcome guests.

Chocolate cake with cup of tea
Makes strange Eucharist for me
Odd temple a field of wheat
Yet consecrated by the feet
Of those remembering days past
When crops no longer last.

ON THE EDGE

I sit upstairs, in my room,
And am sad in the gathering gloom,
A lonely old station I dread,
The last time making a tutor's bed.

To my special friends, farewell,
I still succumb to the spell
Of your presence, and know
That precious memories give me a glow.

Goodbye to Ballycallan and Father Dan
A broth of a boy, fine lump of a man.
I hope that his feet will remain in the clay
That covers the rocks, down Skibbereen way.

Goodbye to the slippers of Peter the head.
To Anne, Brian, Dorothy, all of whom led
My eager steps of years gone by
And helped me flap my wings, and fly.

My wish for the groupies who joined up today –
Be true to yourselves, come what may,
The Truth will always set you free,
And Penny's brown eyes were a bonus for me.

Let there be no weeping for my empty chair,
Just make a mad dash to see who sits there,
Male or female, I don't really care,
As long as you do it, with a touch of flair.

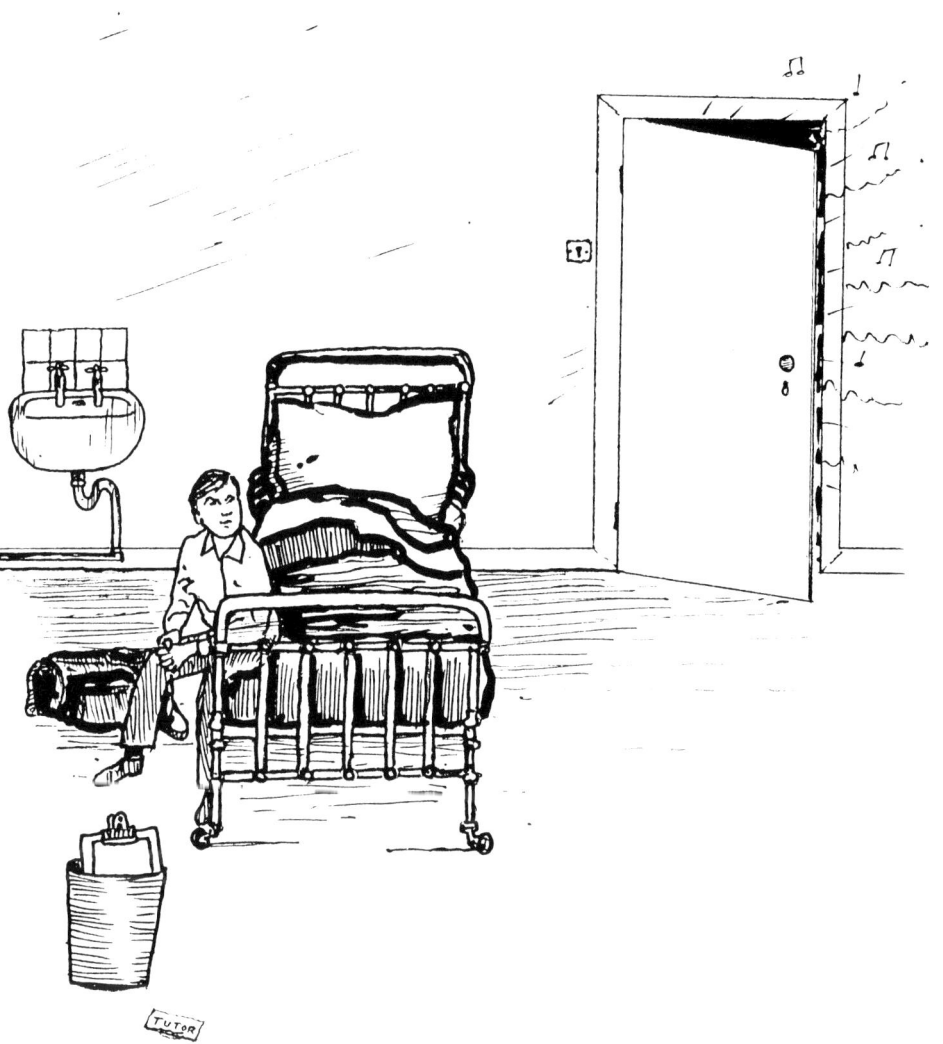

BERNARD FLYNN'S TWO LEGS

The Overseer shouted long and clear
"Flynn, you are skipping Wild Oats, look here,
Young raw townies little know the job,
They are after the handy few bob."

Bernard moved on from Clinton's Hill
To pursue football with Saint Colmcille
Swamped Dunderry with O'Malley
A 'pas-de-deux' of classic ballet.

Meath cheers rang eleven years
Opposition sides reduced to tears
As those two legs with their radar guide
Never kicked any single wide.

The only defence to stop the score
Was to flatten him upon the floor
Which left two very damaged joints
While Staf flicked over extra points.

When fame set you apart from the crowd
The Overseer shouted clear and loud
"I pulled Wild Oats, with famous Flynn,
In that field there, we played to win".

COLM O'ROURKE'S LEFT LEG

Broken, battered, torn, wrapped,
The stands erupted, clapped
Aged leg swung in an arc
History-making in Croke Park.

Missile struck with deep intent
Between the Canal Posts went
The ball with unerring wings
Then the old leg sweetly sings.

When knee cannot bend to pray
There are many who will say –
"Lord, bless that wonky leg
Give it gentle peace, we beg."

WILLIAM

I see you in the lonely grief
Which tears at your Mother's soul
And shakes the everyday belief
That humble faith should be her role.

I feel you in the common sense
Which so marks your Father's way
A strength which can be quite immense
To live and work unending day.

I watch you in the agile brain
Of bigger brother briefly known,
Who feels the loss of buried pain
And finds himself thinking alone.

I sense you in your sister's care
Of little children and their art,
A kind of altruistic flair
And lasting patience on her part.

I smile upon Dearbhla's dollies
While playing house in misty rain,
You'd laugh at the builders follies
Two noses pressed against the pane.

I hear you speak to students learning
Just how to listen and absorb.
Will Doctors be more discerning
Because you came upon this orb ?

I cry, because your life was brief
And many dreams were left forlorn
You would have played behind a sheaf,
And hidden in the field of corn
Yet still I see you all the while
Each time you make your mother smile.

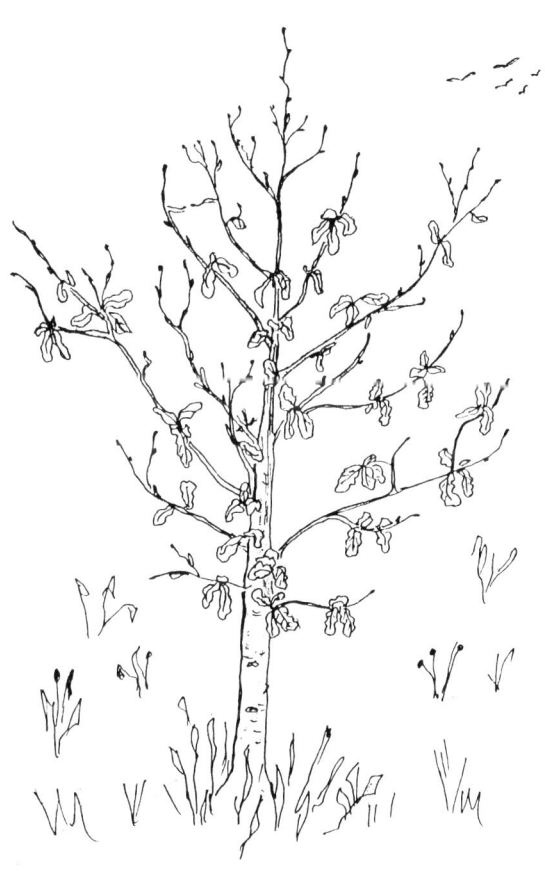

DAYS OF STUDY

I am an inmate of my room
And parcelling out the heat
Will do another sixty minutes
Before I deign to eat.

Books – food – sleep it goes
Luxury is to wash my face,
And seconds stolen from the notes
To ask my God for grace.

Just nine more days are left
To banish chaos from my mind,
Can I really do it ?
Can I true answers find ?

The mountains beckon at the window
Trees and birds a treasured sight,
Monastic walks around the garden
Are the nearest thing to flight.

When that day has come and gone
I will saunter in the city
And watching others try to study
Offer them my gracious pity.

There will be space for music then
And special friends for tea ;
I wonder what possessed my mind,
When I set this goal for me ?

SURROGATE MOTHER

She bit her lip,
And flicked a ponytail
Bag on her hip
And joined the throng.

Home is far away
Strange voices sing
This is my first day
Will I get lost ?

Like picket people standing still
You served by waiting
For the day she might be ill
Or need a friendly fire.

Digs, jigs and wigs have passed
Since last September, years ago,
I called to Mary Mac at last
We had a lot to say.

Surrogate Mother in U.C.C.,
Thank you for odd cups of tea
And waiting for the day,
She had a lot to say.

Where Finbar taught
Let Munster Learn....

'Lucy at UCC'

WEDDING DAY

I bit my lip
And flicked my fringe,
Lucy at my hip,
No time to cringe.

Home is not far away
Strange voices coo,
This is her big day,
Who loses who ?

Like people at a match
All stretched to see
What kind of catch
Mark made in Meath.

Was she a violet
By a mossy stone
Or brightness in the gloom
One way or the other –
She lights up a room.

OTTAWA HILLS

We rode with Johnny to Silver Springs
It seemed a residence fit for Kings
And on his throne, a TV bench,
Sat Russ, who invented the French,
He slept at two, and arose at three
And bought good strawberries for tea.

For there was wisdom in his smile
And he smoked a 'Sure' all the while
That MaryBeth was on the phone
Organising all the world, alone,
She shrieked in the pool age 73
And lost her bag and black coffee.

The green frog squeaked, and Beth came in,
A glamorous granny of my own kin,
She fell for boxes, dolls and bears,
Was hooked on genealogical affairs,
Here is a heart of laughs and pain,
The diet will begin tomorrow, again …

Suddenly, I heard a loud guffaw,
And swimming with fag and a beer in his paw,
The jolly Fritz crashed on the scene
Cracking jokes by Niall Tobín ;
If this is what a Don is like –
I'll join him on the 12-speed bike.

But with no disrespect for him
Cars are provided by Mike, Cory and Kim
And when the pool became too sour
Ben slaved away for many an hour
He left his book at the steering wheel
The Connecticut man is solid and real.

So this is the family we met with Steiff
Something that happens once in a life
May the Lord keep them all on the back of the pig,
And when they arrive at the end of the jig,
I'm sure He'll be waiting with gentle care
And a limited edition of Heavenly Air.

SEA SHELLS

Out at the edge of the sea,
I left my dreams on the sand,
The couples' world forsook me,
Waves washed my empty hand.

Dying every day for years,
I played a game of love,
Laced with my anguished tears,
Crying out to God above.

A dark stranger held my coat,
And his kindness made me cry.
I could either drown or float,
In that black sea, passing by.

I fell in a bog of peat,
On a windswept mountain side.
Old gremlins sucked my feet,
And rescue swallowed pride.

Grappling with my sinful soul,
Dosed on camomile tea,
Struggling to make myself whole,
Seeking the stranger in me.

Out at the edge of the sea,
I watched two shells embrace,
The broken world forsook me,
God's waves brought special grace.

TOM

We laughed loud, and ran away
When you fell into the river
Back in Harry of Beabeg's day
Your wicked face made us shiver.

Years later, when very old
You changed, to work at Beamore
We discovered you were not cold
And had a fund of jokes, galore.

Thin-framed, cloaked in raincoats,
Sucking a precious half woodbine,
Bike grinding, like a mill at oats,
Into the yard, come rain or shine.

Never once a nine to five man
But a tough, live, man, proud of role
And never yet an "also-ran",
A townie with a rural soul.

One day, a brown rat stole your pay
Where I had left it on the bike.
It took a week for you to say
"Where's me bloody money ? Like!."

When you became on O.A.P.,
Still you would blow and puff
There was no need to work for me,
Charlies few bob would be enough.

I said "perhaps you have some needs "
Odd jobs ? To keep your mind afloat ?"
You replied "I'll smoke the weeds,
And Daly's pint will ease my throat ".

"I'll take a spin by Eagle Lodge
And ramble sleepers on the rails
I've spent years trying to dodge
The cowld east wind and the icy gales".

ALONE

Why bother I to clean and cook
Who cares if this is a tidy nook ?
Let papers pile and blankets lie –
Would anyone miss me if I die ?

There is no ear to hear my day
Whether so sad or whether gay –
No kindly arm to hold me tight,
Will this be another lonely night ?

I long to hear a human voice
No longer in books I rejoice
Angry voices could not be worse
Than this sad, silent, lasting, curse.

The world is full of "twos" and "pairs"
I have naught but two empty chairs
Who needs a table, just for I ?
No one would miss me if I die.

My body weary, my soul sad ...
Or am I slowly going mad ?
Must my pillow weep salty tears ?
The fruits of hurt and lonely years.

If someone wrote a letter
Would it break this wretched fetter ?
Can that far distant ringing bell
End this sad, empty, lonely, hell ?

TWENTY-FIFTH BIRTHDAY

Today is the feast of Mary
The fair Duchess of Doner's Green,
And birthday wishes will come by,
From far off folks in lands unseen.

They may be sent by pen and ink
Or just vibration of the mind
"I will not kick up any stink"
Says she "I will take any kind".

Today I have rings from New York
To safely hold my scattered keys
Reminder of the selfless stork
And her driven desire to please.

My old keyring is rather cheap,
So throw it over the wall.
This present gift is a giant leap
From "sales gimmick" to "personal".

Life is made of small wee things
Mice, poems, kittens and key rings
Each has a crucial part to play
As that lifetime slips away.

Why measure span in twenty-fives,
Shorten the gamble of our lives
But in many little acts of love,
A surer way to God above,
Smile on the day and sleep tonight,
Rest assured – the keys are alright.

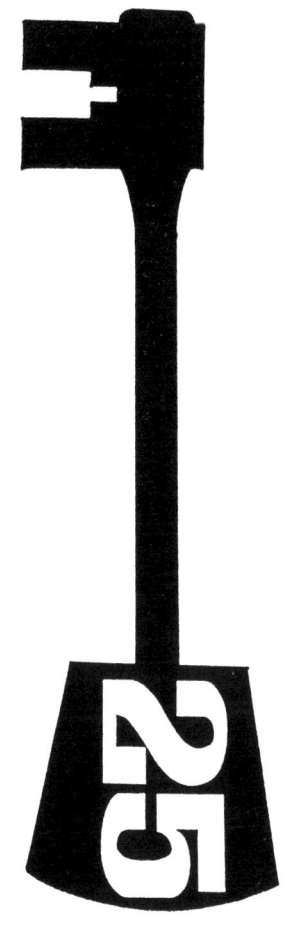

HEADMISTRESS

Pixie curled in a corner-seat
Red and white, with two shoeless feet,
Smiles and tears, mixed together,
In Bellinter's autumn weather.

Willie Telfer for Sunday lunch,
Childhood memory, and a hunch
That something extra special lay
In friendship, on a cold spring day.

Group pent up with deep emotion
Need a kind of healing lotion
We found a mix of smile and tear
That lifted old nightmares of fear.

A normal home of crash and bang
Baby crawled, and daughter sang,
A place for husband to recoup
While big son served a bowl of soup.

For chairing INTO and ACCORD
Some spark must light the scattered word
Despite the damp and cloudy days
This sun warms all with cheerful rays.

Master Mulligan little knew
In school where hedge and pupil grew
His successor would be Anne
Centuries after he began.

A sad boy in a country town
Meets our Pixie with angry frown
His future now is looking bright,
Headmistress Pixie brings new light.

POLYANDRY

Eileen came on the bar of a bike
Fresh and frisky, from an Alpine hike,
Educated by Mother Marie Eustelle
In the hunting lodge, with the convent bell.

She sought a husband in Sarsfieldstown
And married Thomas in a white wedding gown
Leaving the Reverend in U.C.D.,
She threw herself into a family.

Luring Denis from Friesian pursuits
Callan, Lynch and McGrane in cahoots
She lashed around the 10.10.20,
And trees and children grew aplenty.

Next came Edward for a student wife
Speaking Julianstown German, as part of her life
Dealing with students, at home and away,
And Edward himself, in the I.F.A.

Eamon was husband at the famous fondue
Gavin, Dara, Kate and Aoife slept through
The whack of the boot on the whippets' posterier
As he swiftly made exit to darkness exterior.

All now spraken a similar tune,
Having reached the silver apples of the moon,
The family zeitgeist is bound to last
Where a genetic group all move so fast.

Twenty-five years after the Elmgrove "do",
We toast the aforementioned crew,
The Golden Apples of the sun
Await your picking – one by one.

TREATMENT AT THE HEALTH-CENTRE

I got a peck in Peter Street
That almost knocked me off my feet;
The traffic stopped, and Tommy stared
Alice gaped and Evelyn glared
My cheek was red, my heart was full
With such a Nurse, could life be dull ?

PETER THE PAINTER

The very rock of sense, we thought,
Named Petrus G. surely ought
To give a strong solid base
And ease the baby's puckered face.

This notion often seemed good
As long as free from coloured food
Which caused you to run at rocks
And empty out your money box.

The aim to be so artistic
Was long hidden, then ballistic,
When Eustace gave the shop a lick
You took over the old Mähl stick..

Your works look down on London Town
And protect the Queen's best blue gown
Winking at the Hon. Lord Mayor
And Charlie Parnell standing there.

Monks on margins of Holy Kells
Listening for a sound of bells
Or even a Brushfest brother
Could all happen like each other.

With new articles for *SIGNCRAFT* penned
 You always seek the rainbow's end
Someday you will hit the Lotto
And 'rocklike loans' will be your motto.

THE OWL AND THE PUSSYCAT

The Owl and the Pussycat went to Emmaus,
To drink Arthur Guinness, and sharpen their claws,
Found that the groupies liked creating a fog,
Leaving one duo, wading deep in a bog.

There was shedding of tears, unloading of fears,
And jumping to whips from wicked overseers,
Yet always on hand, somebody with a stick,
To pull them to land when murky mire grew thick.

On day three, they waited, with suitcases , in dread,
Each, in trepidation, inside her head,
When hugs revealed that they played the same tune,
The Owl and the Pussycat danced by the light of the moon.

THE NEW CURATE

I met him first, in sixty five
Young, gangling, smiling and alive,
Pouring tea with strong, black, head,
The while we ate Monsignor's bread.

Paddy was shipped across the sea,
While Loughcrew hills were home for me.
He dealt with all the cares of life,
I got used to a brand new wife.

When we got in the chosen few,
Father Paddy turned up too,
We debated by candlelight
When married couples thought they were right.

The Centre flourished, CMAC grew
Paddy poured the odd glass or two
To the team who did P.M.C.,
Managing to serve freedom and tea.

Odd Bishops fluffed the Tuesday game
While God's apprentice made his name
Building a parish by the sea
With lots of help, from Miss Bridgee.

Now we lose a man in a rush
The sea left in horrid nonplush
We'll be welcome in new presbytery
His Reverence will pour stiff glasses of tea,
We had a feeling he would go far,
So watch out, my Lord Bishop, he is on the road
                                to Mullingar ….

LIGHT IN THE SKY

You lived amongst tall trees
Always smiling, ready to please
To mind, to wash, to clean, to cook,
You had a special, sparkling, look,
Until Death came, one winter day
And almost blew the flame away.

You lay sick amongst more trees,
Unsmiling, anxious, ill at ease,
Managing, one day, a slow walk,
Listening to my gossip talk
Stumbling on stony, ancient, stairs
Burdened with sad, childhood, cares.

You searched deep in minds and ways
Building an attempt to raise
Once more a sparkling shaft of light,
To clear the darkness of the night
But often came clouds of black,
Threatening ill to take you back.

You jog amongst the leafy trees,
Smiling, wiser, and well at ease
I, too, travelling, am wiser, now
Old God no longer wants a row
Poems of peace, writing and truth
With sparkle, new, again, like Youth.

A NEW PAIR OF EYES

I watch the world through eyes of blue
And get a different, wounded, view,
Of those who live behind a fence
And lack a world of common sense.

I smile upon the College crowd,
Their newness blows away the cloud,
Which lurks above in Grafton Street
And there is lightness in my feet.

I live once more with desk and flat,
With pen and books, and all of that,
In a world where pleasure knows it's place
And all things run at student pace.

I weep at times to be alone
The party scene is not my own,
And often wonder what lies in store,
When Time will close the College door ?

I thank the Lord for eyes that see,
Through tears, this new side of me ;
That lilac bush beside the gate,
Has now assumed a higher state.

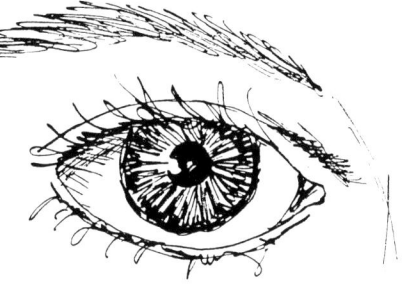

GRATEFUL

For the salt of your tears
And the sharing of fears
The glimpse of your soul
And the making me whole
The way you beguile, and
The warmth of your smile
I am grateful.

A counselling session
A bit like confession
Yet more like a prayer
For the two gathered there
Approached with such love
I am sure God above
Is grateful.

Friend for all that you do
To dispense healing brew
And the lift that you give
So that people may live
With more peace than pain
When they come back again
They are grateful.

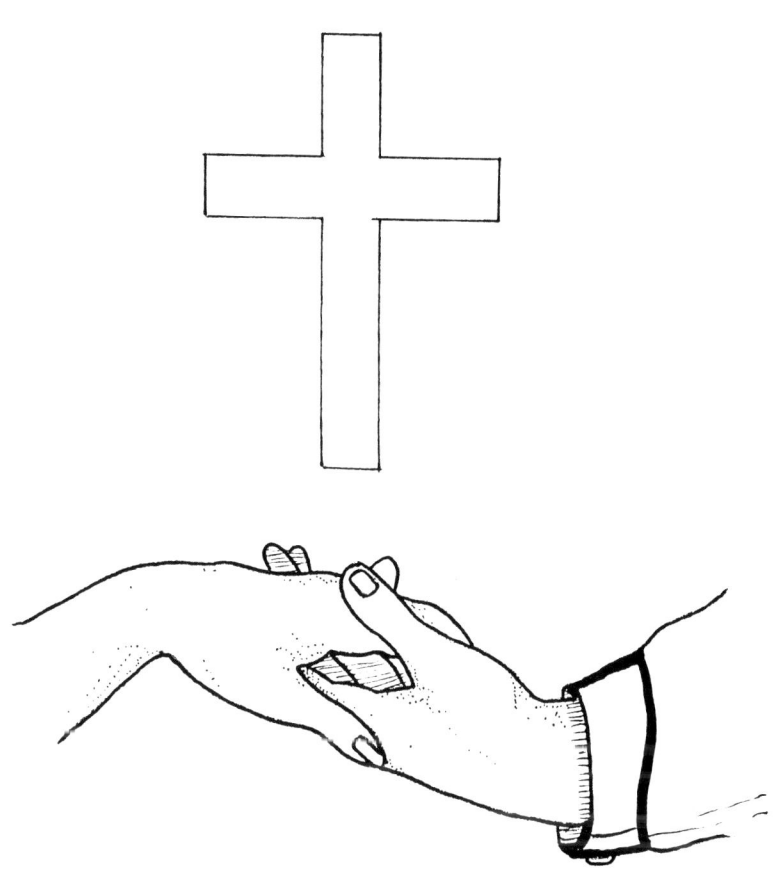

THE WHITE RABBIT

You came at first against your will,
A white rabbit, hurt, broken, ill,
Torn by guilt and spurred by fear
A sad face with a secret tear.

Where is my airy fairy flown ?
Where is the joy she used to own ?
Whose is this shout across the grave,
To force me from a sad enclave ?

I need some space to find a cure
Oh! Mind, why are you so unsure
There is pain in all my thinking ;
I can feel my body sinking.

Do I really love, or do I care ?
Can I ever hope to share
A life of someone close and dear
A loved one whom I do not fear ?

My list to dress the new-found flat
Is torn and tearstained, and ends at that
My heart is also strained and torn,
For every second seems forlorn.

But yet my wings begin to flap,
Philosophy fills the lonely gap,
I find a car, and lamp for bed ;
Is a new me, rising from the dead ?

The broken dream has made me grow,
What lies out there I do not know
Risk the dark with my friend, J.C.,
And know that He'll take care of me.

Broken rules made the Guru grow;
Wounded folk are able to show
A Chinese wisdom by word and pen
That creates knowledge over again.

My thanks for all the feelings shared
I'm glad you know that someone cared,
I've gained as much as you from me,
Found a friend and a cup of tea.

May dreams of Village Life come true,
May lonely moments be so few,
That Love will find a mirror there
Someone to say and mean "take care".

AN IRISH COLLEEN

One sunny Sunday in seventy-six,
Sunnyside School hosted a quare old mix,
Come for selection by C.M.A.C.,
One a ringer for Nana Mouskouri.

Many long years before, a red lad came
Still playing the Normans conquering game
Delacy marched from Armagh City,
Complete with notions like Walter Mitty.

He stopped the long march at Abbeyside
And carried aloft a blushing green bride.
This trim little lady was borne away,
Enjoying each minute, from Dungarvan Bay.

When Brookville Park semis began to grow
Many clever couples seemed to know
And hastened home across the briny sea
Settling in Drogheda, with a family.

We all presumed, on that Selection Day
The sheepskin wool coat would give her away,
And when she lectured long on divorce,
Decided her chances were getting worse.

The ways of God are strange, and not man's ways,
Returning to train, in cold autumn days,
The Brookville trio had settled in,
With fags, and much chat, and the old sheepskin.

This little dynamo started to hum
And an awful lot of good work got done
Approaching each job like a Norman attack
Even the Mylie was taken aback.

Schoolkids and couples, marrieds and singles,
Even wild counsellors, who write jingles,
Were helped along the hard road of life,
By this smiling, working, mother and wife.

In eighty-four came the power of the Chair,
And still she managed with her own flair
To keep a hot temper, and care for all,
And organise well, the Annual Ball.

Retiring now, as a youthful granny
We are certain there are oh! So many
Ways to pursue your favourite hobby
Killing the fleas on your old pet, Bobby.

Full marks, Colleen, for playing lead role,
Which lifted many a saddened soul,
We are glad you got through in seventy-six,
Life would not be the same, sans Brookville chicks !

Thank you, Colleen, for all the care and love,
You have channelled to us from up Above,
And for the strong coffee in the Gables,
While Hugo was selling sticky labels.

LADY IN RED

In a Limerick hotel, late night.
I watched you make the tables right
For breakfast. Answering for my sin,
To Countymen, I churned within.

My moment to pounce had come clearly
That Autumn. Did Presidency dearly
Mean much to me ? Would I follow Greene,
Maher, Clinton, Rea or be a has-been ?

You smiled, and lit the candlelight ;
I struggled with decision that night,
Lady in red, when I left for bed,
You did not know the decision made.

You still live somewhere, but unaware
That history brushed you, lightly, there
In that diningroom of the hotel,
Presidency and I said 'Farewell'.

RENEWAL

Fly high, little bird, with your mended wing
Free to soar above everything,
Cured of the hurt, yet scarred for life;
Living means more than pain and strife,
In the eye of the storm, a gull can glide
While strong men bolt the door, and hide.

TO JOE REA

As a small boy on Stephen's Green
You quizzed your father on the scene
'Are black people the same as us ?'
All the one, and divil the fuss.

The cows in Cahir give milk all white
Yet some have coats as black as night.
When I am dead, and with the Lord,
Let 'fair and just' be your byeword.

A Macra man down to the toes
(not very far from bridge of the nose),
So hard to keep out of the news,
For radical, challenging, views.

Uncivil servants found you a scourge,
So did the Minister, set for splurge,
Even Co-Ops became New Age,
As farmers read the Milk League page.

Tough, pushy, with no time for fags,
Cant, humbugs, or gift lucky bags:
Bertie's P.R. ran into the wall,
Your reign brought consensus to all.

Public persona measuring pence,
Still had a side gifted with sense
For kind deeds and ways to survive
Threats to a farm staying alive.

Fortified by well-buttered toast
The ice-cream dish you liked the most
Travelling the World in search of truth,
Pen ready to strike, just like a sleuth.

Some day you will retire, from minding the garden,
Oldcastle Co-Op will grant you a pardon,
The cows will compute their own Winter fodder
Your house will be trendy, down by the Dodder ....

PENNY

Before you were born, we searched the papers,
Worthy successors to Jesssie we sought,
Each new phonecall the start of odd capers,
Colour, sex or distance, ended at naught.

Suddenly, there was a lead to Kildare,
Under the shadow of Carbury's rock,
We found you gambolling down the stair ;
Two sisters with wall eyes, were a shock.

We did not need documents to recognise
That you were clearly a Protestant pup,
The Pennefeather line was in your eyes,
Of fading gentility, but well brought up !

Colm carried you home in a red basin,
Lifting you over all bumpy feelings,
To preserve your tender stomach chasing
Loneliness, in the County of Kings.

Grown big with R.C. dog food you relax
And sit akimbo, waiting to worry
Electric blankets, crocus bulbs, grain sacks,
Cats, and cartons from the milkman's lorry.

TO SEAN BOYLAN

I watched Heffo steal our pride
In fifty-five, and Freaney hide
It in some secret place, sky blue,
Leaving a Royal crown askew.

A brief time in the sixties with Red
Brought back our belief from the dead,
Once more the flag of green and gold
Flew proudly, as in days of old.

In eighty-two, we had a need
For someone to inspire and lead ;
"I'll fill the gap", said a mild man,
With a bottle, hurl, and no real plan.

We lived lives and moments free
While you slaved at sand and sea,
Hill of Tara, muck, weeds, and frost,
Building a team at personal cost.

Moulding a mix of skill and flair
With individuals tough and rare
You started sharing out the spoils
And gave back distinctive Royals.

Memories, humour, fair comment,
You crafted, with a special bent
And yearly emissaries sent
Taking pride from a skyblue tent.

Great survivor, man of mystique
"effin druggie" in cool dubspeak,
Wise bottler of an ounce of praise,
You brought us joyous, heady, days.

TRAVELLING AUNT

Now Towell was a soldier from Somerset
'But, please, Auntie Mary, could we ever get …'
After the Rosary, child, let us begin,
There's a few trimmins, we have to fit in.

Now a Darcy from Platin came from Dunmoe
'But, please, Auntie Mary, this time can we go … '
Not without sunhats, down to the field of hay
You could just catch cold in the sun today.

Now Cromwell brought in a fellow named Naper
'But, please, Auntie Mary, what was a Flapper ?'
Well young idle women with nothing to do … ,
As I said, he settled down in Loughcrew.

Now, the Rath's have a fishcart in Clogherhead
'But, please, Auntie Mary, all fish tastes like lead …'
Never mind, child, we'll have some in milk today.
I'll make a nice stew, still fresh from the say.

Now the Boss used to go to Doctor Chance.
'But, please, Auntie Mary, did you have romance ?'
Tush, child, I looked after the two men
They needed cooking and minding, now and then.

Now the bowsies haven't sent my dividend
'But, please, Auntie Mary, can we have a lend …?'
You wish to buy comics or books in the shop,
Of course, here is a florin, watch out for Pop.

Now Taaffe, evicted from Sillery's places,
'But, please, Auntie Mary, can we go to the races …?'
Don't be gambling money, watch for Delany,
He will win on the strand, sunny or rainy.

Now, Patrick McCullen, weaver, lived in Beabeg
'But, please, Auntie Mary, what's wrong with your leg ?'
I slipped one wet day and fell in the rain,
The broken right hip never came right again.

Now, Hanrahan's Tinkers lived at the crossroads
'But, why, Auntie Mary, do you give them loads … ?'
Hush, child, I'm just giving some little aid
The children are hungry, I need some tins made.

Now Ninch was a fine place when Grimes was alive,
'Oh! Auntie Mary, see the taxi arrive …'
Well, bless my soul, indeed, what you say is true,
I almost forgot, I am off to Kilnew.

"But, please, Auntie Mary, tell us family links
Before you go off in the big Hillman Minx
Despite all you've said, we need to know more
How did all these Ancestors get to Beamore ?"

NEIGHBOURS

Chance caused us all together,
Like leaves in windy weather
True human choice played no part
Nor did deep feelings of the heart.

Still we have a common root
Of lands, culture and pursuit
Of water scheme, and Colmcille
Of bikes straining on Stubbs' hill.

Old men said 'You need neighbours
More than cousins in your labours
Be careful never to reject
And give them daily all respect'.

Cattle breaks on Sunday morning
Or fire sweeps without a warning,
When thugs rob the private castle
Neighbours help to sort the hassle.

We float into each other's day
Sometimes on purpose, sometimes stray,
Leaves that fall in windy weather
Warm each other when together.

QUALIFIED

Waiting for eighty-four years
You arrived, with a smile,
Some people had joyful tears
We had names to reconcile.

Old folk would have Assumpta
But we had fixed on Ruth
"Protestant name", said Dymphna
"Don't care" said I in my youth.

A dry, sunny, August spell
And cattle needing water
I almost fell in the well
On the birth of my daughter.

Strange how like the well you be
So reflective, still and deep
Petite, bundled, energy,
Thorough in the crops you reap.

Like the original Ruth
In ripe fields of harvest corn,
You have shown eternal youth
And great loyalty since born.

Saviour of drowning brothers,
Embarrassed U.S. Cops
Seen the wide world of others
And charmed the yanks in shops.

Now adding Galway's Irish Gown
Standing lightly at the start
Of career five … any town
Would welcome you to it's heart.

ACCEPTANCE

To carry a friend part of the road
Is not really a heavy load,
Even when the body feels like lead
And things are addled in the head.

Could a fairy be a heavy weight ?
Even at night, when the hour is late
If lesser item want that space,
Your plea is still a saving grace.

Limits of Love can just be set
By the giver of Love, and yet,
We often fear a generous deed
As if it threatened souls in need.

So when the coal and briquettes come,
Out of the blue from thoughtful Mum,
Do not hesitate, take the gift,
Some future day, balance will shift.

Love is giving, some of the while,
And <u>taking</u>, with a cheerful smile,
The giver may be more in need
And your acceptance pays for the deed.

WELL DONE KATE

Is this the wee girl who painted the gates
And herself with the black brush as she went ?
Little knowing then the plan of the Fates,
Unaware of all that artistic bent.

Is this the wee girl who stayed up late
To transcribe for me the long dishrag poem ?
Lately become a more scholarly Kate
Researching and studying many a tome.

Is this the wee girl who pulled the Wild Oats
Observing rootlets, stem and hairy seed ?
Is she now a student with Biology notes
Seeing an organism and not a weed ?

This is the wee girl become a young dame
With good honours, she was a great poocher
But still the kind heart and smile are the same
May she be content in the future.

REGRETS ONLY

Dear Colm, I'm terribly sad to say,
That I'll miss the 27th of May,
The Groupy Weekend for Tutor people
To help them escape their ivory steeple.

Your charming letter from the Cooley Hills
Was calculated to lift any temporary ills,
Imposed by three weekends away
From farming down in muck and clay.

It has talk of changing mood and gear,
To help us drive on for another year,
Without ending up in a deeper ditch,
Or even discovering a brute or bitch …

There was mention of the terrible 50 per cent
Who married a wife or to the country went,
As a means of being an absentee,
And missing the point in Life's Poetry.

The wee orange Programme
Showing where I am,
Was well laid out, and very inviting
And spiced with the personal writing.

There might be a chance to draw cartoons,
Which would be a thrill for the new gossoons.
To see yapping dogs and matchstick men
And silent priests who say AMEN.

The final call and the pointed hand,
That I must go, for my native land,
And follow the General into Death's jaws,
Was very emotional and made me pause.

Alas, however, my answer is Nay,
The cattle might die while I'm away,
There isn't much point in advanced empathee
If cattle are learning R.I.P.

While I'm away in Drumcondra emporium,
The Beamore barley might get Rhycosporium,
And wheat get covered with yellow rust,
So I'm sad to say I simply must.

The Poetry of Love suggests that I stay,
At home with Ann and the gang today.
So have a good old session or a bit of a ball,
God bless you all – until next fall.

DODO

Didus Ineptus – extinct bird,
Was a story I always heard,
And even stood in Jersey Zoo
Where stood a stuffed one, too.

The wings were small, and did not fly
There was a spark within her eye
That could have fired the Jungle dark
And lit the whole of Pearse Park.

Instead of wings, many years flew
And two wee babes to big men grew
Sustained by the singing sisters
A balm to cure life's blisters.

One day, only she remembers
A wand waved o'er the embers
And like Phoenix from the ashes rose,
Arrayed in beauty and new clothes.

Didus Ineptus, extinct no more
With graceful, feathered wings that soar,
Above problems of big five-O
Have a lovely day. Do-Do.

MOVING

I came, in halves, unwanted, small
My brain in a sea of scatter ;
New people risked their all
And old trainers did not flatter.

Pain was around the walnut tree
Practice in the Tallaght tower,
And oft I heard the lonely plea –
"How did I get in with this shower ?"

Now, I go, with new friends blessed
A suitcase, plant, and watch so true ;
Even pigs would find pastures new,
And supervise all of the rest …

GOODBYE HEALTH CENTRE

I lost them all in just two days
Without much time to say goodbye ;
Yet I was glad in some strange ways,
There was no time to break, and cry.

Farewell to the strange unhappy dame,
Who cast Dean Swift upon the flame.
Farewell, Old Barney, black with fire
And rough hands cut with dalky wire.

Farewell to the sweet blind woman
"You were bigger, at first coming"
Farewell to muddled mothers fuss
"Nuss, the child is sick, Nuss, Nuss, Nuss ......"

Goodbye, glass box with stony views,
And Porter Paddy's nose for news.
Goodbye, green cards, the pile that fell
Can just lie there, or go to hell !

Goodbye, Alice, a lady fine.
To all the babes I felt were mine
Goodbye great men, whose souls did fly
Part of myself, with each did die.

I feel like some Quasi Modo,
Losing a lifelong heavy load O,
Like a convict freed of ball and chain,
I now can try to walk again.

Even though the hump and chain be gone,
I find it hard to feel alone ...
Like when clouds have passed away,
One does not trust a sunny day.

Out there is a sea of little eyes,
Filled with hope, love and surprise.
Help me, Good Lord, with all these chaps
Chart new waters, and make new maps.

BEST BOY IN THE SCHOOL

Look at the screen, watch the bearded head
"HERE IS THE NEWS ... BY DERMOT", it said
"MAN HITS LAMP-POST WITH CAR" ... then you grin
"TAKE FIFTEEN" – DERMOT !! STIFFEN THAT CHIN!

"Mister, Missus – this boy is a pleasure" –
Overworked teacher gave a measure
Of his relief at the human race
Turning out one, with an ideal face.

Robin Hood swung about in the wood
Killing the sheriffs, saving the good
Enrobed in sheets, raising the chalice –
Ideal material, free of malice.

Speaker in Louvain, painting the mural
Rattling off "A"s – single and plural
Only "B" on the paper for Art ?
Call an inquiry !! Who lost his chart ?

John Boyle O'Reilly - a particular joy,
Auditor, Musician, Milkwood boy,
Neolithic man watching the sun,
Singing in Carberry's, just for fun.

It's hard to be all things at one time
There is truth in Pat Ingoldsby's rhyme
Stop the world – paint long ladders and snakes
We'll get it perfect ... at sixteen takes.

TO THOMAS CLINTON

A young man with an aching back
Yet managing to cram and pack
Several lives with crises stuff
Four at a time never enough.

Sole-farming from the age of five
No one could say you weren't alive
To new technology. They say
'try Paddy fields in Dundalk Bay'.

Thus Land Tax came and Land Tax went ;
Much credit goes to you who spent
Many hours playing right notes,
Finding places with marginal votes.

You were King of hardship cases
With disease and money, - oasis
Of hope for families in mess
Helping Banks dispose of largesse.

A Leader who ran with the ball
And Beggy – like would sometimes fall
Or gain an impossible score
When hope had vanished out the door.

One fatal day, you made them choose
Which way of life they wished to lose,
And thus began a long campaign
You fought in trenches, might and main.

Presidents come and Presidents go
When history judges it will show
Clinton an honourable man
Who dealt in commerce with elan.

FREEMAN OF KELLS

Uncle Dick is coming today
The Monsignor is on his way
Speaking Latin or Ancient Greek
I wonder is he just some freak ?

Let us sit on Cunningham's wall
Carve wooden whistles for you all ;
Do you really drive motorbikes ?
Could you put engines on our trikes ?

The Bishop said 'Records must burn'
I wonder did that make you spurn
Bishops hats forever after ?
Did Kells offer Stoic laughter ?

V.G. dressed in blanket coat,
Deep voice rumbling in your throat
'Come in, and have brown bread and tea',
Fear'd by Bishops, Uncle to me.

Building churches, homes and schools
You broke all the closed shop rules
Cleared sewage, fixed the heat
Carved turkeys and were discreet.

At ninety-three, nuns made a cake,
Refusing, you gave orders – "Take
It to savages where I was born,
They'll show more respect, than scorn".

Now you say "it is time to go"
Young and foolish, I tried "No"
"Knox's big book has still to be read
Before it is over, I'll be dead".

My will is cheerful, nothing dark
Books to Maynooth, name to the Park
When you hear the ringing of bells
Say farewell to the Freeman of Kells.

Bury me amongst my own Kells folk ;
Then up the People, and they spoke
"We need you at the Churches wall
Kyrie Eleison on us all".

SESQUICENTENNIAL

What on God's earth do you want to do ?
Bring all together Old James' crew ?
After a century and a half,
Well … perhaps it might be a good laugh !

Mark, Anne, a Committee of Whizzkids ?
Well … O.K. … I'll give you the quids …
Who was it now ?   The chap she married ?
What was the baby's name she carried ?

A Mass at the gatehouse, in the bleach ?
How far will the cable for the mike reach ?
Helen, where will we get a fiddle ?
Father Dick, please stand in the middle.

The bales would feed well in Boherard,
Any chance of a load from the yard ?
William ! Garlic bread is my desire,
Desist ! My love, the house is on fire !

Barry and Billy, please stop fighting –
We engage in debate, enlightening.
Did you ever see Guides with attitude ?
Blame James and Ann, if you think them rude.

Maria and Dermot, talented twins
Belting out numbers to see who wins
Thos. wants a photo at the front door
Of the Hartlands return to Beamore.

It is one of those memorable days,
When hearts are warmed by strong sunrays,
Windows on genetic material
Make a special time-ethereal.

Speeches and chat laced with good wine
Momentoes, trees, motorbike combine
With kinship and welcomed inlaws
Not to mention overworked jaws.

Neuro-Linguistic Programme, you think ?
Exactly that, can I have a drink ?
Young Paddy is a poet, so am I ;
Toast Joan's bouquet, until we die.

SICK CHILD

I sit, and watch my little one
Surely more could be done
To know the cause, or ease the pain
Why does it have to be me, again ?

Please, God, make Jenny right
I'll take her place, for I can fight.
Please let her jump and cause me strain
That is so little compared to her pain.

My eyes escape the head so worn
And wander to a field of corn,
Faraway on a summery hill …
Oh ! Why does my child lie so ill ?

Please let her make a horrid face,
Or even at my back grimace
When the child did something bold,
Why did I ever shout and scold ?

Crash, clatter, more visitors come,
The child awakes, she is not at home,
The fretting starts, the leg can't bend,
Oh ! When will this nightmare end ?

They are gone … I am left, so thin,
Both hands fix twixt belt and skin ;
I'll eat when I see the x-rays,
Tomorrow or the next day, the Doctor says.

Night is coming, and fitful sleep,
Perhaps it will become so deep,
To let me homeward make my way
And snatch some rest ... to face the day.

Creaks the door, flashes the light,
Nurses must change, for the night ...
Mammy, Mammy, where are you ?
Here, my love, what can I do ?

I wonder am I fair to Kate ?
Playing at home, outside the gate,
Or to the sick child who needs my care,
Oh ! God, is this to be my share ?

Forgive me, Lord, I'm knackered, you see,
Why did you send this cross to me ?
To bear alone, and the pain to endure,
Of others I love, and cannot cure ?

Jesus, come, and hold my hand,
Listen to my heart and understand,
Provide a Father for evermore –
To our little Stranger on the Shore.

CHRISTMAS

Alone, with thoughts, on Christmas night
No normal hug to hold me tight
It would be so easy to feel sad
At times when duty says "Be Glad".

My children slumber with their hope
Desperate … in the dark … I cope
Lord, must it always be this way,
Me, on my own. At close of day ?

Somewhere, within my trembling soul
Like a mare nuzzling a baby foal
An unseen touch has turned my eyes
To gaze upon the eternal skies.

There, is a bright and shining star,
Whose light has travelled from afar,
In time, as well as frosty space,
That light has shone on God's own face.

Connected to the light above
With God, and people, that I love
No more alone, on Christmas night
But hugged in that eternal light.

THE DUSTER

A sudden, unexpected, call,
Breathless, you came into the hall
Moved the rug, opened the lock,
Oh ! John, come in ! This is a shock …

You sat in sofa, softly spoke,
As if from slumber just awoke,
Duster placed in a firm grip
Reticence in your lower lip.

This pretence lasted for a while
And then you melted with a smile
Removed the duster to one side
Revealing what you tried to hide.

A torn knee in faded jeans
Quite normal to a man of means,
And so, from out a cloth of dust,
Comes a new and deeper trust.

HANDYMAN AVAILABLE

This supervision is worth a lot
I intend to use what I'm sure I've got
I'll check the assumptions at the very start
And practice is the basis of any Art.
A twinkling eye and a gentle ear
Will help to banish guilt and fear
And when I get stuck – and can't see the way
To God and the Group - I'll pray.

A MOTHER'S LAMENT

With happy heart, my soul doth sing
Blow the trumpet, let joybell ring
My firstborn child in my body grows
Enjoy our time, before the world knows.

I see this child, from foetal screen
A tiny heart, it's beat serene,
Confident, and utterly new,
This the creation of me and you.

Days pass into weeks – wonder grows
And yet the pace of heartbeat slows
Oh! God, the hours seem so long …
Is there something awful that is wrong ?

Hold on, my child, hold on to life
What can I do to help your strife
As tiny fingers grasp the thread,
I am helpless, blind, in fear and dread.

It is over … and all is still
My God has gone against my will
Your little life has graced it's stage,
Why you ? Why me ? Why us ? I rage …

Friend, listen, as you walk along
For our first baby's precious song
Watch a flickering in the night,
Before the darkness, before the light.

CONFERENCE '83

I sat in Registration Hall
And gloried proudly in it all
A job well done, and no complaints
From crowds who were no bunch of saints

The beds were booked,
The meals were cooked,
Fees collected,
Speeches dissected,
Posters on the wall
Order, King of all.

Suddenly, into selfish pride
Intruded your sad face which cried
"I'm going home, I cannot stay –
This place is driving me away!"

"I'm lonely in this caring crowd,
The groups, tea breaks, are shouting loud
'Go home now, you do not belong',
The Bishop sang a thoughtless song".

"Why are the tables made for six?
Why don't I fit into their mix?
Please get a lift to my hall door,
Off this Institutional floor".

I brought you out with heavy heart,
Moment of triumph torn apart,
Monarch stuck to my stupid throne
Empathy fizzling – on it's own.

I wondered did you know or care,
And yet, you had come to me to share
That moment of extreme distress
When life seemed a total mess.

The one who works her soul away
Also needs a special time to play ;
The nurse who bears a lamp of love
Needs fuel to light, from here and above.

INSTALLATION AID

Farmer John, I sentence you to doom
Said the wise Professor, in his room,
Surrounded by academic books,
To me in the field, circled by rooks.

Five gloomy sentences in a life
Of farming, was it eternal strife ?
And whither move Global food prices
In which the W.T.O. rejoices ?

They dance upon a greasy tightrope
Who entertain such devious hope
When one twin has vicious hunger pain,
The other stuffs his belly, again.

Root researchers charge sizeable fees
To build up branchy Family trees
While you sit under the selfsame wood
And wallow in soft ancestral mud.

Five wide furrows earthed by the plough,
A farmer guides his tractor now
And then his classmates all officebound
Envy him his hallowed piece of ground.

Planting seeds in a carpet of clay
While commuters squirm for half a day,
The wind gently whistles through the leaves,
And feet are flexed, for traffic heaves.

Crops and cattle are a fence away,
Chips and softwear both require L.A.,
Flights, Brussels overnights, Heathrow trips
Skimming fields with Brussels sprouts in chips.

The combine sings it's way through straw,
Birds warble, and Penny licks her paw
Childborne lunch trips lightly thro' the fields,
And on the mad motorway, no one yields.

If this remote life appeal to you,
Slow down your pace to a cow cud chew,
Mix some animals in with the plants,
And find a group free of sycophants.

COWPATH

Winding through the long grass
Changing tack each year
Whether a route to Mass
Or water for the steer.

Bare birthplace of mushrooms
Gives ease for the stumblers
Way home to the handlooms
Kicking place for grumblers.

Remnant of the Stone Age
Dynamic route of feet
Decipherable page
And where two lovers meet.

Harvestmans starlit trail
Struggle for the wee child
Carrying food and mail
Dodging tall thistles wild.

Rope on the Master's waist
Cast in the Divine plan
Time granted, just to taste
An Angelus, for man.

TOUR OF '85

One showery day in sodden July
Accidents happened both you and I
That landed us on a tour of Louth,
Unnoticed duo in an aged crowd.

We were labelled at Rokeby Hall
Whose solid design amazed us all
Cars moved off, like a pack of hares,
And moving still, we were left upstairs.

Next shower came in Protestant pews,
While we examined Anti-pope views,
The prototype church for all first fruits.
God's place for all saints and some galoots.

Then hunger called at Clogherhead,
The picnic lasted till we were fed
With coffee, chicken, peach in it's skin,
And Maureen, standing with the biscuit tin.

Rambling on to the Lodge of the Seer,
The oldest house at the edge of the mere
Phillistines ran to examine inside,
But we postponed, with time to bide.

This meant rambling midst Tichbournes flowers,
Rather, I felt, like Eden's bowers
With exotica here, rare plants there,
And little homebound clippings to spare.

The rustic summerhouse kept us dry
And cadaver tombs remind us why
We are here at all, to reach above,
Searching for an everlasting love.

Shuffling slow the oldest Beaulieu floor
We saw paintings in miniature,
Side by side, with the Swanzys and Yeats
Nudes, King Billy and Drogheda's gates.

Farewell, Nesbit and her Ladyship
The votes of thanks that easily trip
Off tongues ancient, very loud,
No rogue Republicans in that crowd.

We sauntered the avenue in style
While others walked in single file ;
A thunderclap, and the rain did lash,
Saunter changed to a headlong dash !

Farewell my friend, who shared my day
Much thanks for kind friendship on the way
The tempo of that tour will still last,
When all the old artefacts have passed.

EXAM WISH

Good luck today with your pen and brain,
Throw yourself at it, with might and main,
May the head stay clear, fresh and free,
You can be sure of help from me.
It is meant to be a happy day,
So read the question, and blaze away.
Read the question a second time,
If for no reason but to rhyme,
And then apply the Golden Rule
Read it a third time, keep your cool !

KILSHARVAN

Gravestones and builders brought me here
Catching fingers, I shed a tear
In pain, at the lid of the old car ;
Why did he leave the thing ajar ?

The monks arrived to sing of John,
Bitter-tongued, and carry on
A Christian song and burial mound,
On Armstrong's 'tasteful bank of ground'.

House stands o'er the River Nanny
Soldiers, Doctors, Lawyers, many
Other folk from the linen trade,
On these old banks good livings made.

A tulip tree of age unknown,
Surrounded with sweet flowers, grown
By green fingers, of long before,
Stands sentry at the pillared door.

Tall ghosts from out an Antrim glen
Mix with the ancient milling men,
And tough ladies, prepared for wars,
Mix Cof-O-Era in the jars.

Farewell, Old House, you change mistress
And leave those going in distress
But bringing memories on their way
With which to bless the Narroway.

SHARING

How can I share you, with the world,
And often seem so cold
To leave a space, with easy grace
For other eyes to hold ?

Candles lit are not for hiding
Nor gold for miser's grasp
Love is free, and all – abiding,
And owns no mental hasp.

When love makes flower blossom touch
And cause your smile to grow.
How, when you have shared so much,
Could I want you, for show ?

Brief moments come for us alone,
Watching new blossoms grow,
We possess a common vision,
That love means letting go.

THE QUEEN OF BROOKVILLE

'Twas long, long, ago, I first met Tess
And sold her cookers for more or less
Six a penny for Maggie Dolan,
Better to sell than have them stolen.

After England, and after Big Jim
We were brought together by a whim
Of some pushed priest, who needed names,
To play Sunday selection games.

Three musketeers arrived sheepskinned,
One talked, one smoked, one just grinned;
She did not lecture, had no degree,
But was wiser than a Ph. D..

Thus was she cast, to be the Mammy,
Burst on stage, with Betty and Tommy,
And now appears – almost Nationwide –
The knitting mother, by the fireside.

She laughed and sang, for Fianna Fáil,
And cheered up Charlie, and us all,
And 'tis only God himself would know,
The people that she helped to grow.

To live by love was her only rule,
Yet known to have the kick of a mule
In her alter Ego, Mary Ann …
She was a great match for any man.

But the role she played with most success,
Was just being wise and kindly Tess,
For this we all live a better life …
Thank you, Jim, for the loan of your wife.

GLENCRAFF

Now, Sir, do you see that green patch
Backing to the mountainy hill ?
Sure the door will be off the latch
And Jane standing, welcoming, still.

No such thing as a mearing fence
Between mountain, bog or neighbour,
But lines of poncans making sense,
No capital replacing labour.

Weathered men work by the boreen,
Tossing turf in Tullyconor,
Waiting, watching for young Maureen,
With a timeless sense of honour.

Running water on the mountain,
Electric current soon may come,
Clear and cool as from a fountain,
Nice to have when the girls come home.

A gale coming back from Salruck,
And Peter gone … gone on the boat
Surely we are due bits of luck,
But ,God, I have lumps in my throat.

John Joe gone too, only died once,
I'm glad the boat wasn't his choice,
Time passing is now at nine months,
Poor Rex comforts me, which is nice.

Back to home, and die in the bog,
I have buried four men given me.
What matters now the rain and fog,
Let me prepare my soul for Thee.

SISTERS

Out of the hidden, deep, black, gown
Came an apple to lift my frown.
For knees cut on a rusty nail,
Medical skill prevented jail
In a hospital bed. The mail
Brought a pincushion, without fail,
A gift from old feeble fingers,
And in the choir splendid singers
Of Jahweh, to make statues cry,
When the old P.P. came to die.
Dry August days and Convent tea,
With a china cup, just for me.
An angry nun, of years fourscore,
Grateful for Family at her door,
Ready to kick for Liverpool,
And even bend the sacred rule.
Generous soul who gave a roof,
Warm and loving, never aloof,
Open to embrace, without fear,
While watching schoolgirls raise a cheer.
Leading the Church, with common sense,
And courage, courage … so immense …,
Pushing the limits for the sad …
Knowing these nuns has made me glad.

THE EGG

This gift has flown the sea
Picked with thought and care,
Packed with gentleness and flair
And proudly given to me.

It has to be a living sign,
A simple mealtime thing
Yet with a strong symbolic ring
And happily 'tis mine.

It gives much pleasure to mine eyes,
And sitting by the ticking clock,
Pray God that none will ever knock
This lilac coloured prize.

ENERGY

There is an energy in Love
Which lifts the mind to things above
And causes thoughts to teem around
Like May grass growing from the ground.

Teeming thoughts are oft forgotten
Like August grass, growing rotten,
Clogging growth of fresher thinking
Each leaf on the other sinking.

So. When a Love creates new shoots,
If I am loving to the roots,
I harvest what the sun has made
An energy that will not fade.

A HOOLEY AT 40

There is a hooley for someone on tonight,
It is in the nice house with the purest light
Where you will always find types of river rush
And Tod, the wee mongrel, eating his mush.

Please ring the doorbell, try it several times
For it does not always peal it's chimes,
But keep persevering and you will soon hear –
Beethoven's sixth, or ninth, float on your ear.

If, perchance, there is an absence of Adam's rib
Wait for the Maestro, with the brush in his bib,
He will regale you, with a pot of Earl Grey –
"Oh ! I think Mary is gone to do schools today".

She is terrible busy, with baskets and things
Rita is coming to paint, and Tess has got wings
From her last novena to Saint Augustine
She fed them ice-cream and the kids are bustin'

Crash! Clatter! Bang! Our winsome, fair, lady comes,
In from a night's yoga, with several chums ...
"I have to run out now, to Father Tom's youth,
Because Ancestor Bacon told me, forsooth !".

There are six people ringing, to offer jobs,
But heaven provides, God sent us a few bobs.
Do you know what it is, I'd far rather be
Mothering at home, with the fabulous three.

I do not feel at all as old as they say
Born on the feast of Matthias today.
The door of the car – it no longer needs twine –
For a generous man said it is all mine.

You have found the hooley for precious Mary
Let us all celebrate with the Towell Fairy
We do know we are welcome, healthy or ill,
To the four decade lady, on the old hill.

A MAN APART

Stopping on the road to Kinnegad,
Wondering what Gavin Halpin had …
What spirit did he leave in Fair Street
For Rhona, myself and Margeurite ?

Could it be his Jesuitical looks
That made us read spiritual books
And left him with an ever-open mind,
Gently tolerating all mankind ?

What caused his enigmatic smile
Was it summer spent on Western Isle
Or scattered family of ten
That would have bothered lesser men ?

Perhaps a plot laid with Dorian Grey
To camouflage his old age away
And always have a fresh, youthful spark
Instead of being an ageing nark ?

The Oilcake people gave him a chair
What strange symbolism was buried there,
That, after a lifetime as the Boss,
Even the workers felt at a loss ?

In Ancient Ireland, things came in three's
And now my mind clicks o'er with ease
I have found the legacy of three
Which Gavin gave to other men and me.

The first is his independent view,
Courageous, logical, clear and true,
The second, the way he left us free
To learn for ourselves, Ann, Donal and me.

What final gift did he leave to us ?
I hear you ask, on the snowbound bus,
The third is something very serene,
Smiling and strong, who else but Aileen ?

VINCENTIAN

Woven like a sacred, golden, thread,
You brought prayer to bless the dead ;
A golden priest from '33',
Part of a living tapestry.

When I gave Ann a golden ring
You blessed a hidden, deep, down, thing
Which started at Saint Stephen's Green
And gave us inner strength, unseen.

Raising the family cup of gold
You lifted spirits, young and old,
Landing in planes from God knows where,
You left us gifts of precious ware.

Sometimes a card from Mozambique
Or tapes from Rome to hear you speak,
M.H.F. to reverend Daughters,
Over mountains, land and waters.

A public person for the Vins
Lifting people in their own skins,
Halting traffic in clammy Rome
Intrepid guide to Peter's Dome.

Yet in all of that priestly role
The nearest touch of noble goal
Comes in visits to lonely beds
Stitching peace with God's golden threads.

PASSING OVER

Will I die in a field of grass,
Or on a distant mountain pass ?
Or fade away in an aged bed
With nurses fussing at my head
Or with love to hold my hand
In my own place and native land.
Wherever it be, O Lord, I pray
Give me the peace I feel today.

LEGACY

When I am gone, will you carry on
And listen to my spirit's wish
As if I held your hand,
Come from some promised land ?

I'll need some limbs to move about
And fill a busy day,
A speaking voice, to smother doubt,
And spread hope, on the way.

Your smile can move the dark
As if I held a light,
And shining eyes provide the spark
To lift a soul in plight.

My gift to you will be much peace
With love to give away
And laughs to bring you ease,
Upon a lonely day.

So when I am gone, will you be wise
And cast my cloak for me
Since even an angel in Paradise
Needs love to turn the key.